REFLECT
His Character

As an elder, are you living a holy life?

REFLECT
His Character

jim estep, david roadcup, gary johnson

COLLEGE
PRESS

Foreword

What would our churches look like if we all had godly, scriptural elders who were all about serving and following God's will? What if our elders were transformed to be solely men after God's own heart who worked for His Kingdom at all times, in all ways? Can you imagine a church led by men who are true followers of Jesus Christ and carry His cross daily, sacrificially dying to self and serving with agape love?

You know, I can't think of a more important area in the church than eldership. When "the elders ain't happy, ain't nobody happy!" The elder board can make or break a church staff or even the church in general. If the elders don't work well with the Senior Minister, life can be unbearable for both. But on the other hand, God-ordained leaders can create an atmosphere ripe for our Lord to grow a church into just what we read about in the book of Acts.

I am really excited to see this series of publications. It comes at such a great time in the life of our church here in Louisville. For the past several months the elders at Southeast Christian Church have been defining their roles to make sure we are being as true to Scripture as possible. The question this series hopes to answer is: "As an elder, do you sense it's God's will for you to serve?" It is our desire to respond a resounding "yes" in complete confidence as we continue to see what the Lord has for us here.

How much churches would gain by utilizing an effective, God-filled elder selection! This is certainly an individual process for each church, but how many churches simply appoint those who tend to work the longest or ask the loudest? The Bible is full of qualifications that are ignored or tweaked in order for us to appoint just who we think we want in the role. But don't be drawn offside. What mistakes we make when we leave the Lord and His word out of the equation!

Elders are certainly not perfect, of course, but that is one reason they are able to help others through adversity. They have learned to use for Kingdom work what they've been through to grow others. They have the maturity and character to step back, pray, and courageously speak up, as well as work through conflict to become the leaders they've been chosen to become. But the key is the divine call—that nudge the Lord gives to passionately lead and serve in any way He sees fit. Do they live the word? Do they know the word? Are they ready for the overwhelming assignment they've been given? I pray they are—and with God's help, the insights of this publication can certainly improve the process and transform the world.

I'm anxious for each of our elders to read this series and talk about the implications. These books will truly be used of God to equip our congregational leaders to be ready for the role they have been assigned. But as the authors remind us, transformation of our elders must begin individually in the heart of each.

I can't wait to see what the Lord has in mind to transform our churches throughout this series of books. I've known Jim Estep, David Roadcup, and Gary Johnson for years. Their integrity makes the lessons and insights come alive even more. A huge thank you for tackling a topic we all think we know so much about, and yet I feel that, through these publications, we will be given the knowledge to help open the door to the great power of scriptural eldership.

Dave Stone, Senior Minister
Southeast Christian Church
Louisville, Kentucky

Table of Contents

Introduction

Do you ever go stargazing? Have you ever spent time staring into the night sky, or used a telescope for a closer view? Amazingly, the moon at its brightest has no light of its own, but simply reflects the brilliance of the sun. Similarly, we are only able to see the planets because they reflect the sun's light. They are reflectors of that which they orbit. *So are we.* Our lives reflect what is at its center. What is it that you orbit? What is your life's center? We reflect the character of whatever is in the center of our lives. When others look at you, do they see the character of our Father? "Be imitators of God, therefore, as dearly loved children and live a life of love, just as Christ loved us and gave Himself up for us as a fragrant offering and sacrifice to God" (Eph 5:1-2).

Healthy congregations require a healthy leadership. Without a healthy leadership, the odds of a congregation growing spiritually, let alone numerically, are greatly diminished. This is the principal concern of this series: Healthy leadership facilitates healthy congregational life. To ensure healthy congregations, we must give attention to the health of our leadership, the elders. This book endeavors to orient, inform, challenge, educate, and ultimately equip men to be leaders within the congregation, elders that genuinely lead and shepherd the flock of God. It calls us to reflect in our character the character of Christ while serving as elders within His body.

Leadership that is Christian is based on God's *call* to service, one which we must *Answer*. The man is qualified and equipped by a life representative of Christian *character*, maturity; we *Reflect His character*. Further, an elder must possess *competencies*, abilities that serve him well as he leads and shepherds God's people; *Lead* His congregation.

Finally, the *community*, both the congregation and its social context, provide the area for an elder to serve as a leader within the community of faith and a witness to the community around it as we *Enjoy* His people. All four are essential for Christian leadership to be effective, none of them are optional.

About the Series

This book is the second of a four-volume series on the leadership of elders in the congregation that will be released by College Press over 2009–2011. The four volumes (*Answer, Reflect, Lead,* and *Enjoy*) parallel the four basic components of Christian leadership previously explained. These books are not intended to be scholarly treatises of the eldership. Rather, they are designed as useful study guides that utilize practical and academic insights to provide a "manual" to the **These books are not intended to be scholarly treatises of the eldership.** eldership. Each chapter is intentionally brief and concludes with reflective questions for your own personal use, or use as an eldership as a means of training and equipping one another for service.

Reflect, Volume 2, addresses the character of an elder as a leader in the congregation and community. Chapter 1 asserts the necessity of a Christian mind among the eldership; one that has been transformed by Christ and no longer conforms to the world's pattern. Chapter 2 addresses the spiritual lives of elders, asking them to reflect a growing relationship with God, with Chapter 3 addressing one key element of spiritual life, prayer. Chapter 4 is on protecting one's character, with recommendations on how to avoid burnout or spiritual and moral failure, while Chapter 5 addresses restoring one's character and the character of others, with an emphasis on confidentiality among the eldership. The final chapter discusses the value and importance of having elders accountable to other elders, spiritually and pastorally.

This book can be used in two ways. First, it can be used as an individual study, something that you as an individual elder within the congregation read for your own edification and education. You may be a new elder, or perhaps an experienced leader looking for additional perspective and insight. As such, each chapter includes Reflection Questions designed to help you apply each chapter to your life as a Christian and an elder. A second way in which this book can be used is by your eldership. Each elder could read the book, and use the Reflection Questions both individually and to discuss the text together as an eldership. The six chapters could be part of six elders' meetings, or even used in a leadership retreat as a means of sparking reflection, discussion, and application, with the book's theme becoming the theme of the retreat. In either case, whether individual or group, we do hope the book is beneficial to your life and ministry.

About the Authors

This series is not the product of one author. Rather, it is the fruit of three individuals' labor, working in concert with one another, and bringing their diverse experience and perspective to the table for discussion. One of the authors is a churchman (Gary Johnson, left), another  is a church consultant (David Roadcup, pictured here with his wife Karen), and still another is an academic (James Estep, right). While these three men have known one another separately for a long time, it was not until they were all three together in Heiligenkreuz, Austria, teaching students from eastern Europe and central Asia at *Haus Edelweiss* (TCMI) that the three men sat together for the first time and shared their concerns for the health of congregations and the health of its leadership. We are convinced that a healthy leadership builds a healthy congregation. From these

We are convinced that a healthy leadership builds a healthy congregation.

initial conversations over coffee a hemisphere away came the idea for this series, designed to strengthen the health of elders as the congregation's leaders.

While individuals were assigned their own chapters to write, the final form of each chapter was reviewed and reworked by all three authors sharing a common table, typically in Indianapolis, Indiana. Hence, the work is a tri-authored resource for the equipping of congregational leaders who serve as elders of the Church.

We are praying for you and your congregation, and if we may be of service, feel free to contact us at your convenience. **July 2009**

James Estep, Jr., PhD
Professor of Christian Ed.
Lincoln Christian Seminary
Lincoln, Illinois
jestep@lccs.edu

David Roadcup, DMin
Director, Center for Church Advancement
Cincinnati Christian University
Cincinnati, Ohio
david.roadcup@ccuniversity.edu

Gary Johnson, DMin
Senior Minister
Indian Creek Christian Church
Indianapolis, Indiana
GaryJohnson@TheCreek.org

Thinking Character

James Riley Estep, Jr.

"I love you" written in gold foil upon a box curiously shaped like a heart. Cards with bow-wielding angelic babies releasing arrows toward the hearts of wanted suitors. There was a time when people believed the heart, or even the bowels, were the seat of the emotions and intellect. After all, your heart races, slows, skips a beat, or even aches given your situation. However, these are simple reactions to what the brain is processing. We have known for centuries that the brain is in control. Just as all roads once led to Rome, everything goes back to the brain (but giving brain-shaped boxes of candy may not be as appealing). In fact, of the five senses we possess, four of the five sensors themselves reside within inches of it (eyes, ears, nose, tongue), and all five are processed by the brain. The brain is also the container of the mind, our thoughts, dreams, ambitions, values, priorities, knowledge; even faith—all of this resides in the mind. But have you ever thought about your thought life?

Paul wrote, "The mind of sinful man is death, but the mind controlled by the Spirit is life and peace; the sinful mind is hostile to God. It does not submit to God's law, nor can it do so" (Rom 8:6-8). Who, or what, does your mind reflect? What is at the center of your thought life?

There is a reason this book starts with a chapter on the thinking-character of an elder. The mind is the center of all other character matters. We live out what our mind is thinking! Even our body is simply doing what our mind tells it to do. This chapter concerns itself with the seat of our character: *the mind*. D.L. Moody once wrote, "Character is what you are in the dark,"[1] where no one can see what we do, where we are alone with only ourselves. This is the case when we consider our own thoughts. This chapter will discuss the character of a Christian mind as described in Scripture, particularly for elders as congregational leaders. It will also address how our thought life is reflected in our character, how others see our thoughts through our lives. Finally, it will provide a plan for cultivating a Christian mind. It will call for the transforming of our mind into the mind of Christ, as exemplified in our character.

> **The mind is the center of all other character matters.**

Mind in the Character of an Elder

It is easy to say that mature believers should possess a "Christian mind" or the "mind of Christ," but what does that mean? Scripture describes the mind of the believer in numerous passages, each one giving a new dimension to the Christian mind. With each dimension, however, comes a cautionary tone against those elements that may thwart or cause a Christian to stumble. As we think of our thought life, we must first affirm what God expects the Christian mind to be or become.

James warns his readers, "That man [one who doubts] should not think he will receive anything from the Lord; he is a *double-minded man*, unstable in all he does" (Jas 1:7-8 emphasis added). Notice how James draws the connection between being double-minded and living an unstable life! If our mind is not given wholly over to God, what foothold are we giving to others? Regardless of what we may think, we must center it on God. Even in matters of opinion, Paul contends, "One man considers one day more sacred than another; another man considers every day alike. *Each one should be fully convinced in his own mind.* . . . If we live, we live to the Lord; and if we die, we die to the Lord. So, whether we live or die, we belong to the Lord" (Rom 14:5,8; cf. 1 Cor 7:37-38). For us, as Protestants, we do not believe in the sacred versus the secular, but rather that all truth is God's truth and all thought must be centered on Him, wholly. Otherwise, we may deserve the same rebuke given to Peter by Jesus, "Jesus turned and said to Peter, 'Get behind me, Satan! You are a stumbling block to me; you do not have in mind the things of God, but the things of men'" (Matt 16:23; cf. Mark 8:33).

I live in the country and use well water. We also use a water filter. It removes the impurities from the water, making it more palatable for my family and useful for cooking. The mind itself is a filter. It determines what is acceptable, favorable, important, etc. In a Christian context, the filter is for the purpose of purity. For example, Jeremiah frequently expressed his commitment to God, saying that a given thought "did not enter my mind" (Jer 7:31; 19:5; 32:35). However, Paul provides another model of filtering, one

The mind itself is a filter, determining what is acceptable.

saying, "We demolish arguments and every pretension that sets itself up against the knowledge of God, and we take captive every thought to make it obedient to Christ" (2 Cor 10:5-6). We all live in the world, but we are not to be of the world (1 Cor 5:10). I cannot expect to be totally removed from the world, but I can make sure the world and all that is in it is subjected to Christ in my mind, and life.

> **Reflection Question:** Is God in your thoughts? If one were to observe your behavior or listen to you speak, how would this be seen in your character?

A Spirit-controlled Mind

Who is in control of your life? It is a myth to believe in our own absolute autonomy. We may be in control of our lives, but not total control. Paul asserts that we are simply in control of who controls us. He writes,

> Those who live according to the sinful nature have their minds set on what that nature desires; but those who live in accordance with the Spirit have their minds set on what the Spirit desires. The mind of sinful man is death, but the mind controlled by the Spirit is life and peace; the sinful mind is hostile to God. It does not submit to God's law, nor can it do so. Those controlled by the sinful nature cannot please God. You, however, are controlled not by the sinful nature but by the Spirit, if the Spirit of God lives in you. And if anyone does not have the Spirit of Christ, he does not belong to Christ. (Rom 8:5-10)

Paul asserts that we are simply in control of who controls us.

Does your mind reflect the control of the Spirit, or of your flesh?

Paul does not end his affirmation here, but later in Romans he further contends,

Therefore, I urge you, brothers, in view of God's mercy, to offer your bodies as living sacrifices, holy and pleasing to God—this is your spiritual [Gk. *logikós*] act of worship. Do not conform any longer to the pattern of this world, but be transformed by the *renewing of your mind*. Then you will be able to test and approve what God's will is—his good, pleasing and perfect will. (Rom. 12:1-2)

Paul uses a different word for "spiritual" in Romans 12, *logikós* (from which we get the word *logic*), one that reminds the reader that part of our spirituality is our mind; and that conforming our mind to the Spirit is to be transformed from the world.

Paul sounds the caution of having an unspiritual mind. He cautions the Colossians, who are in the midst of heresy, "Do not let anyone who delights in false humility and the worship of angels disqualify you for the prize. Such a person goes into great detail about what he has seen, and his unspiritual mind puffs him up with idle notions" (Col 2:18-19). The spiritual mind is one that is transformed from the world, that reflects God's will and not his own; one that pleases God, not self. Charles Spurgeon wrote, "Character is always lost when a high ideal is sacrificed on the altar of conformity and popularity."[2] The spiritual-minded elder realizes that he cannot be controlled by himself, but by God. It is a matter of placing priority in the Spirit or self: will we be controlled by faith or fear?

Reflection Question: What (or who) is in control of your mind? When faced with a decision or predicament, who do you reflect, God's Spirit or the weakness of your flesh?

A Wise Mind

In the Old Testament, Solomon calls his readers to wisdom and understanding in life (Eccl 2:3; 7:25; 8:9,16), demonstrating the connection between wisdom in mind and life. Scripturally, wisdom is not a matter of earning a university degree or possessing certificates, but a maturity of knowledge that translates into practical living, represented by a character that is covered by godly wisdom. It requires one to move beyond a mere knowledge or acquaintance with Scripture, but to develop a comprehensive view of life, a mind-set that is consistently reflecting on one's living. How is this achieved? While living wisely is something for all Christians, it is particularly necessary for those who lead. Paul encourages the Philippians saying,

> Finally, brothers, whatever is true, whatever is noble, whatever is right, whatever is pure, whatever is lovely, whatever is admirable—if anything is excellent or praiseworthy—think about such things. Whatever you have learned or received or heard from me, or seen in me—put it into practice. And the God of peace will be with you. (Phil 4:8-9)

Your mind is shaped by what is put into it! In turn, your character is shaped by what is in your mind. As Charles Reznickoff wrote, "The fingers of your thoughts are molding your face ceaselessly."[3]

Living wisely is particularly necessary for those who lead.

"Now the Bereans were of more noble character than the Thessalonians, for they received the message with great eagerness and examined the Scriptures every day to see if what Paul said was true" (Acts 17:11-12). This is quite the contrast when compared with Paul's assessment of Roman culture, writing, "Furthermore, since they did not think it worthwhile to retain the knowledge of God, he gave them over to a depraved mind, to do what ought not to be done" (Rom 1:28). Nothing could be more noble, right, pure, or praiseworthy than the continual study of Scripture and from this the formation of wisdom in the life of the Christian. As an elder, wisdom is essential, not optional. If we are to demonstrate a thoughtful character, it must be evident in our lives and first present in our mind.

Reflection Question: How well do you live out Scripture? How well do you integrate the thoughts of your mind with the way of your life? How great is the gap between the two? What areas may need attention in this matter?

An Eternally Purposeful Mind

I remember the first time I ever saw a real 3-D movie. It was one thing to view a movie in two-dimensions, against a flat screen and at a distance; but it was a completely new experience to view the movie with the 3-D glasses, or put into a large concave screen, thinking objects were coming out of the screen toward me. It added a whole new dimension, one that a two-dimensional movie could not provide. For the Christian, eternity is the added dimension. We view life through a different lens, one with a dimension that is not considered by those outside our faith.

Paul writes, "Since, then, you have been raised with Christ, *set your hearts on things above*, where Christ is seated at the right hand of God. *Set your minds on things above, not on earthly things.* For you died, and your life is now hidden with Christ in God. When Christ, who is your life, appears, then you also will appear with him in glory" (Col 3:1-4).

Christians prioritize eternity, and reprioritize their life with eternity in mind. This produces an incredible life change. As C.S. Lewis penned, "If you read history you will find out that the Christians who did the most for the present world were precisely those who thought most of the next."[4] We begin to invest our lives in more significant activities, not the daily or routine concerns of this world or our own lives, but invest ourselves in the lives of others and become purposeful in our commitments. This is seen in Scripture when the phrase "having in mind"

God's intentions are unchanging, unlike man's.

denotes intention, *especially* if the Lord is with him (cf. 2 Sam 7:3; 2 Kgs 10:30; 1 Chr 17:2; 2 Chr 7:11-22; Matt 1:19; John 6:6). Why? Because God's intentions are unchanging, unlike man's (1 Sam 15:29), and hence He gives purpose to our lives and to our work beyond our lives.

It is for this reason that the New Testament condemns mindless religious practices, those that seem to lack purposefulness and lead only to fruitlessness. For example, in introducing the model prayer, Jesus says, "And when you pray, do not keep on babbling like pagans, for they think they will be heard because of their many words. Do not be like them, for your Father knows what you need before you ask him" (Matt 6:7-8). Similarly, Paul questioned the Corinthians' inappropriate use of tongues saying, "For if I pray in a tongue, my spirit prays, but *my mind is unfruitful*" (1 Cor 14:14). Our character should reflect the eternal dimension of our thoughts, and be exemplified in the causes to which we commit our lives; with minimal interruption from the world.

Paul's letter to the Philippians, which was specifically written to the elders and deacons of the congregation (1:1), makes the affirmation, "Then make my joy complete by being like-minded, having the same love, being one in spirit and purpose" (Phil 2:2-3). Even when a congregation is divided, such as the problem-plagued Corinthian congregation, the injunction is to "be of one mind" (2 Cor 13:11). While our thoughts are our own, they ultimately belong to God. When a congregation, or an eldership, is like-minded, their sense of purpose and relationship are self-evident. An elder who has an eternal purpose in mind reflects this in a character that is intentional and deliberate, and willing to sacrifice the temporal for eternal concerns.

Reflection Question: Watch the www.youtube.com clip entitled "Attention Test." (It's actually called "Test Your Awareness: Do the Test.") It is the one with basketball players. Just watch it! [READ NO FURTHER UNTIL YOU HAVE WATCHED IT.]
Were you amazed? Did you miss it? Tell me, what is it that you focus on so intently that it causes you to miss God in your life? What distracts you from viewing life from an eternal perspective?

What comprises a Christian mind? Four simple, but profound, principles comprise the mind of a mature Christian. It is a mind that (1) is centered on God, not the world; (2) is controlled by the Spirit, not the flesh; (3) exercises godly wisdom, not foolishness, and (4) is purposeful for eternity, not entangled by the temporal. With these four components in place, a mind devoted to Christ guides the life of the elder, and is seen in his speech, commitments, decisions, and behaviors. However, how do we form a Christian mind?

Cultivating a Christian Mind

"I just got back from Vegas!" Immediately stares, muffled conversations, and either smirks or raised-eyebrows are observed. I get that a lot. Lincoln Christian University has an extension site in Henderson, Nevada, next to Las Vegas, and I frequently fly in on a Thursday morning to teach Thursday night and return Friday morning. I am there about 12 days a year with that itinerary. I actually enjoy Vegas! When I'm there, I fellowship with students both inside and outside of class, visit with others from our host congregation Central Christian Church (a congregation of 17,000+), and have an opportunity to share with friends.

However, there is another side to Vegas. As I drive down the Vegas Strip (Las Vegas Blvd.), I see two worlds: unparalleled architecture, fantastic landscaping, and amazing shops and restaurants. . . . And then the other side of Vegas's reputation enters view: rampant gambling, "shows"—I'll leave it at that—and the promotion of activities that do not deserve mention. How does one maintain a Christian mind living in such a culture? How can we cultivate Christian leaders surrounded by such an enticing venue?

Cultivating a Christian mind is essentially a three-phase process (Figure 1.1), each with its own practices. It may be as simple as the old saying, "Garbage in, garbage out," but it is indeed a matter of having concern for (1) what goes into our minds, (2) how it is processed in our mind, and (3) how our mind is expressed and thus seen by others: reflecting a character of blamelessness, above reproach; a consistent character that always reflects a Christian mind.

Mind's Input   Mind's Output

Elder's Mind

Figure 1.1

Mind's Input

"Watching TV doesn't have any effect on me!" Sure, that is why billions of dollars a year are spent on commercials. "Listening to that kind of music doesn't make me think about anything!" Yeah, that is why even more billions of dollars are spent on creating jingles and catch phrases. We are in a constant stream of input through our senses. Images, sounds, words, and sensations bombard us daily. They are inescapable.

So, do we just shut off everything? Like the desert fathers, should we move into a desolate region, away from culture and society? No. We cannot stop reading, watching, listening. This would indeed not be healthy to our mind, or our spirit. However, we must be aware of what is going into our mind. We must also be capable of assessing what input is beneficial and what is harmful to our Christian thought-life. While it would be advisable to have a steady mental diet of Christian materials, such as biblical study, Christian books, movies, and music; we need not be limited to strictly Christian items.

We must be aware of what is going into our mind.

We need not limit our mind's input to only items from a Christian perspective. Paul said, "whatever is true," etc. Paul himself demonstrated a familiarity with non-Christian literature (Acts 17:28; Titus 1:12), but used for Christian purposes. As Christian leaders, we should demonstrate a maturity of mind that enables us to be thinking Christians, not ones ignorant of what is happening beyond the walls of the church. However, as Christians, we cannot find value in certain input. For example, pornography is not justifiable for any reason. Once those images enter the mind, they are there, permanently. This can lead to disastrous effects on one's life. Similarly, Scripture warns us. "Nor should there be obscenity, foolish talk or coarse joking, which are out of place, but rather thanksgiving" (Eph 5:4-5), and that joking is often a means of deception (Prov 26:19). Making such topics as sexual conduct, racism, or any sin a matter of jok-ing *can* lead to our being desensitized, not taking it serious-ly, and allowing it to enter our minds without due consid-eration. It is almost impossible to "unlearn" something, and so we must be on guard about what we allow to enter our thought-life. Hence, we must take care of what we allow to enter our thoughts, and ultimately what is expressed in our character.

Elder's Mind

Input is only the beginning. How do we process what we learn, what we see and hear? Just what should go on in an elder's mind? Whether the material be Christian or not necessarily Christian, we need a process whereby to appropriate and make the most effective use of our learning. The processing of the mind's input explains how it will be used, and how much influence it has on us. Perhaps asking five reflective questions will enable us to process the mind's input most effectively:

> **We need a process to make the most effective use of our learning.**

1. *How does this bring glory to God?* Some inputs may be more readily applicable to this than others. But the more one has to rationalize how something glorifies God, the more suspect it should be considered.
2. *How does this compare to my theological convictions?* Everything is theological! Nothing should escape a theological assessment, and so any new input should be filtered through a theological lens.
3. *How does this add to what I already know?* As a matter of processing new information, determining in which "file" it belongs or if it constitutes something entirely new is rather important. It also ensures that new learning will be integrated into existing learning.
4. *How does this feed my spiritual walk with Christ?* Asking this question aids in making use of new information as a means of Christian formation. New input may provide new perspective, new means, or new insights into our spiritual lives.
5. *How does this aid my leadership as an elder?* As a congregational leader, one must always keep on a steady track of self-improvement. Any input that has already received

favorable remarks from the first four questions should have some impact on your leadership.

Using these reflective questions, along with any others you may want to employ, should provide for the ready processing of new input, but that's not the end of the whole process of cultivating a Christian mind.

Mind's Output

Character begins in the mind. Character may be exhibited by what we say and do, the attitude and values we portray, but all this begins in the mind. Like a young child who just doesn't know that some things are inappropriate to say, what is in the mind usually slips out eventually and unintentionally. I remember a friend breaking out into laughter when seeing a sign in a store. It was an odd occurrence. The sign was not intended to be funny, and yet he was almost giggling about it. When asked, "What's so funny?" he quickly realized that he couldn't explain his laughter without embarrassing himself. It was an obscene comment made by another individual that he had long forgotten, until he saw the sign. Our character is indeed a reflection of our mind. We have already mentioned guarding the input and providing for the processing, but it is also critical to ensure that the output of our mind is pleasing to God as well. As an elder, your thought-life is "public," seen by members of the congregation and read by them in terms of your character. "No one will ever know what I'm thinking" . . . think again; if it is not expressed in your words, it will be seen in your life!

It is critical to ensure that the output of our mind is pleasing to God.

Conclusion

The truth be told: *Vegas is everywhere!* We all live in Vegas! The internet, late night cable channels, magazines and books, and after-hours television programming brings Vegas into our homes, offices, and anywhere a computer screen can be found. We need to be intentional about cultivating our mind in the context of Christ: guarding its input, processing it appropriately, and reflecting Christian wisdom in all that we do as elders. When this is done, we exhibit a character consistent with the content of our minds.

Reflection Questions

Given the pattern described above about cultivating a Christian mind, assess yourself in regard to the following phases (1 being needs improvement and 5 being highly evident):

Mind's Input	① ② ③ ④ ⑤	Explain:
Elder's Mind	① ② ③ ④ ⑤	Explain:
Mind's Output	① ② ③ ④ ⑤	Explain:

Chapter One References

[1] Found at www.christianquotes.com/character (this site now no longer active).
[2] Ibid.
[3] Found at www.christianquotes.com/thought.
[4] Ibid.

The Spiritual Growth and Development of the Elder

David Roadcup

When building a new home, one of the most important facets in planning its construction is the proper installation of the footer and foundation. The footer sits on the ground and is basically a strip of steel reinforced concrete laid out in the shape of the proposed house. The **footer's** width and depth depend on the size and number of floors the house will have. Depending on the house, it can be as thick as one to two feet and as wide as two to three feet. The footer is very crucial to the construction of the house because the foundation and rest of the entire house will be supported by it. This strip of concrete will provide the base on which the entire house rests. If the footer is not installed properly, the house can develop cracks and other very severe structural problems.

The spiritual life of an elder in the church is quite like the footer of a house. As a solid footer undergirds the construction and long-term dependability of a building, so the healthy spiritual growth and development of a church leader mirrors not only his devotion and love for the Lord, but also provides the substance and power for his leader-

ship ministry in the body of Christ. **Formation and depth**
It goes without saying that the for- **of the spiritual life of**
mation and depth of the spiritual **a church leader is of**
life of a church leader is of utmost **utmost importance.**
importance. Personal spiritual growth and development
should be a primary concern in the life of anyone who is
leading the church. It is the heart of the issue when it comes
to ministry for anyone called to lead the body of Christ.
The fact that we are growing, moving forward, and developing in our faith and relationship to Jesus should be, as
elders, one of our highest personal priorities. This concept
should be taught to men desiring to become elders before
they are ordained. They should come into the eldership
clearly understanding that their spiritual lives and personal growth as Christians have a great deal to do with their
leadership of the church. Encouragement in this area
should be ongoing to an already established team of elders.

This chapter will discuss the spiritual life and development of an elder. We will share together in why a deepening spiritual life is important and how elders can grow and
continue to advance on their spiritual journey.

God Calls Leaders to a Journey of Spiritual Growth

Once we come to salvation through Christ and are born
again, we begin our spiritual pilgrimage. It is definitely not
a 100-yard dash, but more like a marathon. We refer to this
experience as a "journey." The apostle Paul refers to the
Christian life and experience as someone's "walk." In Colossians 2:6, Paul states, "Therefore, as you have received
Christ Jesus the Lord, so *walk* in Him." Paul's imagery indicates that as believers, we are to be moving forward, not

standing still. There is movement and action. There is forward progress and life. There is growth.

Reflection Question: What kind of runner are you? How would you describe your spiritual journey?

Growth is normally a good thing. Henry John Newman said, "Growth is the only evidence of life."[1] When farmers plant a crop, the evidence of a positive season is the fact that the crops are growing and there will be a harvest. A couple will tell you of the health of their new baby by telling you that at the last doctor's visit, the baby "had grown an inch longer and put on five ounces in weight." When a new business is having increased sales, there is a spirit of expectation at future success. Growth is a positive thing.

God is calling us to grow in our personal relationship to Him. Just as a parent wants their child to grow and develop normally, so God desires the very same thing for His children. In our context, this is especially true for someone in leadership in the church. Henry Blackaby writes, "Spiritual leadership flows out of a person's vibrant intimate relationship with God. You cannot be a spiritual leader if you are not meeting with God in profound, life-changing ways."[2]

We should define what is meant by spiritual growth at this point. A good definition of *spiritual growth* or *spiritual formation* would be: *the daily proactive development of a passionate relationship to Jesus Christ through growing in love for Him, obedience to Him, and developing fruitfulness in my life for Him.*

The true heart of spiritual formation in the life of an elder comes down to one thing—*growing in my love for Jesus.* As we grow in our love for Jesus, we will grow in our desire to seek Him and get to know more about Him and

His will for our lives. The more we grow in our love for the Lord, the more we will grow in our spiritual walk and our recogni-

The more we grow in our love for the Lord, the more we will grow in our spiritual walk.

tion of Him as the supreme Lord over every area of our lives. We must understand that becoming a believer is not just adding one more thing to our lives. It is not a "compartment" among many different compartments. When we come to faith, Jesus *becomes* our lives. Jean Fleming writes, "Christ must not become simply another item in our life—not even the most important item. He did not come in order to be the most crucial piece of our fragmented life; He came to absorb all of life—our family, job, talents, dreams, ministry—into Himself and impress on it His mark."[3] All partitions are torn down. Jesus is our life (see exercise at end of chapter).

In the process of spiritual formation, God continually guides the believer in his or her pursuit of growing as a Christian. It is man's response to God's leading that produces good things as we grow in our faith.

God's Part

God directs the process of spiritual formation in the life of every believer who wants to grow. In Philippians 6:1, Paul tells us "For I am confident of this very thing, that He who began a good work in you will perfect it until the day of Christ Jesus." The word Paul uses here for "perfect" is the word, *teleios* which refers to something that has grown up, become completed or finished. It carries the idea of something growing to maturity. Paul is telling every believer this: God promises us that just as he began the work of salvation in us at our conversion, as long as we are willing, He will continue to grow and develop us to maturity. In

God is continuously active and moving in our spiritual formation. doing so, He is preparing us for the coming of Jesus at His return. What an amazing promise! God is continuously active and moving in our spiritual formation. We know that He will use people and relationships, circumstances, His Word, prayer, fellowship (our life in the church), the call to personal discipline, suffering, and a host of other experiences to bring us to (*teleios*) maturity and completion.

Elder's Part

An elder's part in this process is to understand and respond to Scripture's teaching concerning a leader's personal spiritual growth. Hebrews 6:1 tells us "Therefore leaving the elementary teaching about the Christ, let us press on to maturity (*teleios*). . . ." In 1 Peter 2:2, Peter says we should, "like newborn babies, long for the pure milk of the word, so that by it you may *grow* in respect to salvation. . . ." Again, in Colossians 2:7, Paul describes us as "having been firmly rooted and now being built up in Him and established in your faith, just as you were instructed, and overflowing with gratitude" (a powerful picture of growth and maturity). Second Peter 3:18 admonishes us to "*grow* in the grace and knowledge of our Lord and Savior Jesus Christ." The request is clear to every elder. God wants us to proactively move forward spiritually. He wants us to leave "spiritual infancy" or "spiritual puberty." His desire for all leaders is that they would seriously move forward in their desire for and quest of spiritual maturity.

In our spiritual journeys, an important question to always ask is "What does God want from us?" When it comes to the spiritual formation in the life of an elder, the following is critical:

1. *God is calling us to love him with all our hearts.* In Matthew 22:34-40, we are told that a lawyer came to Jesus and asked him, "Teacher, which is the greatest commandment in the Law?" Jesus answered, "You shall love the Lord your God with all your heart, and with all your soul, and with all your mind. This is the great and foremost command." The Great Commandment tells us clearly what God wants from us as His children. He wants us to *love* Him. It is interesting that Jesus did not say, "You shall *serve* the Lord your God," or "You shall *fear* the Lord your God"; He said, "You shall *love*. . . ." God does want our worship. He wants our service from pure motives. He wants all these and much more to come gushing up from the deep spring of our heartfelt love for him. It may sound somewhat unbelievable that the great God, this transgalactic Omnipotence who strides the galaxies,[4] our God who holds the universe in the palm of his hand, would primarily desire love and devotion from his human creations. But this is truly the case. We must love our heavenly Father with our intellect in agape love. We love Him with our minds. We should also be developing the emotional side of our love for the Father. We feel a warm and personal love for our spouse, good friends, and family members. This same emotional connection should be growing in our relationship to the Lord. This is all part of learning to love the Lord with all our heart, soul, mind and strength. This is what the Lord wants from us.

2. *God is calling us to passionately pursue Him.* Growing in our love for God definitely involves our proactive pursuit of Him. We run after Him with great intensity. Psalm 42:1 states, "As the deer pants for the water brooks, so my soul pants for you, O God." David, the shepherd, had expe-

God wants us to desire Him; He wants us to run after Him. rienced many Judean summers and their extreme heat. Many of the normal watering places for wildlife dry up during those summer hot spells. David may have actually seen deer that had perished due to a lack of water. David would tell us that just as a deer, desperately searching for water to sustain its life, pursues that water with great intensity, in like fashion a believer intensely seeks after God. It is with that intensity and focus that we pursue God on a daily basis. David repeats his desire for God in Psalm 119:10 when he says, "With all my heart I have sought You; Do not let me wander from your commandments." God wants us to desire Him. He wants us to run after Him. Our heartfelt desire to know God and pursue Him is a part of our spiritual formation.

Reflection Question: Love and pursuit assumes an active relationship with God. What "activities" do you do that contribute to your relationship with God? What activities may impede or trouble that relationship?
• Write three ways to better your relationship with God.
• Write three ways to remove the most obvious impediment.

The Imperative of Personal Growth for the Elder

For his own interior world and his own personal spiritual health, an elder needs to foster the activities and regular practices which will nurture his own walk. His interior life in his spirit needs to be healthy and thriving.

An elder's spiritual roots must be deeply secure in Christ because of the privilege and responsibility of leading the church. Not everyone is called by God to be an elder. When this calling comes, it should be received with great humility and gratitude. Because of the gravity of dealing with the Body of Christ and the issues of eternity with which an eldership deals, the role of an elder is great. There is a certain amount of expectation and pressure on people who are elders that is not found in respect to a layperson. It is similar to James writing in his epistle in 3:1 when he says, "Let not many of you become teachers, my brethren, knowing that as such we will incur a stricter judgment." James was not talking about our judgment at the end of time. He was talking about the judgment and evaluation of our lives by our fellow believers as we share life in the spirit with them. Elders are held to a higher standard. This is clearly seen by the characteristics lists in 1 Timothy 3 and Titus 1.

As elders, we are called to shepherd the flock. We are called to take care of the church and her members spiritually and in other ways. As teachers and leaders, we have to be aware of the fact that we must take good care of ourselves as we take care of others. We must have our hearts tuned to Christ at all times as we are called upon to serve, lead, and make decisions which will determine the direction and future of the churches where we are serving. It is true that as the leadership of a church goes, so goes the church. When leaders are cultivating a deep and rich relationship to Christ, this will be the model and norm for those following. As we teach, we must be well fed and healthy, because it is impossible for us to feed others if we are starving to death ourselves. We can't empower the lives of others spiritually if we are leading powerless spiritual lives ourselves. We can't take people to places of depth if we have, personally, never been to those levels of depth. To lead people to deeper

To take people to places of depth we must have personally been down to those levels.

places in their walk with Christ, we must have tread those paths before them.

Personal, spiritual growth must become a major priority in an elder's life and schedule. Most people today live lives characterized by a hectic schedule where people, events, and commitments scream for our attention. Family events, job, social life, sports, church involvement, etc., crowd onto our daily planners. The issue of time and where we spend it is crucial. Time today is like currency. There is only so much of it to expend. In today's culture, it is sometimes easier to ask people for a financial contribution than it is to ask them for their time. Lots of important items fill an elder's schedule. In light of the time pressure we all feel, an elder must ask himself, "What are the most important things for me to accomplish today?" In the midst of a very busy schedule, an elder must cut time for personal spiritual development. It has to be a priority.

A number of years ago, my wife and I purchased a home in a fairly undeveloped area of a suburb of a large city. In the eight years we lived there, the city grew out around our subdivision. Large, new subdivisions sprang up. Strip malls, gas stations, and movie theaters began to appear. New buildings and developments were everywhere! One day I was driving past a building site and noticed a flatbed truck with a winch offloading a large metal box onto a new concrete slab. The box was raised up from the truck and while being stabilized by several men, slowly was moved from the truck bed to the slab. Jutting out of the slab at exactly the right spots were large bolts. The metal box was lowered onto the slab and positioned perfectly by the men handling it. As the bolts found the prepared slots on the box, it came to rest on the slab. The men then took wrenches and tightened **Elders face the** large nuts onto the bolts, securing the **tyranny of the** box onto the slab. I wondered to **urgent every day.** myself what purpose the box would be. A pizza oven for a new restaurant? I mentioned this event to a group of men in our church. One of the men informed me that he had been working at that job site. He told me that the large metal box was the *vault* for a new bank building. He said that the vault was so large that it had to be set before the framing took place, as the vault was too large to install after the framing was completed. I said to myself, "There has to be a teaching illustration in there somewhere!" The teaching is this: "We should always do the most important things first!" Elders face the tyranny of the urgent every day. With jammed schedules, we continually need to ask ourselves the above mentioned question, "Out of all the important things I am needing to do today, which are the most important?" I would suggest that giving attention to our spiritual growth and development on a regular basis is one of the most important issues we could consider. Later in the chapter, we will discuss details on how to make this happen.

Essential Elements for Growing in Our Walk

Every elder should have an understanding and working knowledge of the key practices, habits, and experiences, known and practiced for centuries, which dramatically contribute to spiritual formation. These are elements which will bring us into the Presence of the Lord, draw us close to the heart of Christ, and direct us into the love and ministry of the Holy Spirit. When practiced without legalism, they are life changing. They are critical to our walk in

Christ. They are the avenues which will stimulate our spiritual walk and understanding with great power and growth. They are called the Spiritual Disciplines. Dallas Willard comments on the importance of the disciplines when he writes, "Full participation in the life of God's Kingdom and in the vivid companionship of Christ comes to us only through appropriate exercise in the disciplines for life in the spirit."[5] Let me say categorically that it is impossible to significantly grow in our spiritual walk without the regular practice of the Spiritual Disciplines. We want to discuss several key ones and suggest how they might be woven into the life's fabric of an elder as he leads in the body of Christ.

The Word of God in the Life of the Elder

Every elder should cultivate the practice of internalizing the Word of God on a regular basis. This is done by reading and thinking deeply on a portion of Scripture each day. It means taking time to consider the teaching and instruction in that passage. When we do this, it is God speaking into our hearts and minds His timeless message. We need to hear from God through His Word. God will meet you there. We need His message each day to teach and inspire us. We need to be reminded about who we are as children of God and to whom we belong.

We need His message each day to teach and inspire us.

A regular, devotional reading of the Word of God does several important things for us when it comes to spiritual growth.

Scripture "Performs Its Work in You" – First Thessalonians 2:13 tells us that the Word of God "performs its work in you who believe." The Word of God works in our lives on a daily basis strengthening us, teaching us, convicting us, feeding us, and encouraging us. It works in our hearts and minds creating in us the Spirit of Jesus. (See 2 Timothy 3:16.) The Word works in us to bring us to maturity.

Scripture Feeds Our Spirits – When we take time for a devotional reading of the Word of God, it does for our spirits what eating a good meal does for our bodies and minds. It nourishes us. It feeds us. It provides strength and stamina for us for the day. This is not just a good devotional thought. Scripture itself uses the following descriptive terms: The *milk* of the Word (1 Pet 2:2), the *meat* of the word (Heb 5:14), solid food (Heb 5:12-14), the bread of life (John 6:35) and the water of life (John 7:37-38). So when we take time to devotionally read a section of Scripture each day, it nourishes us and provides the energy we need to grow in our spirits and experience victory in spiritual warfare.

Scripture Directs Our Lives – Psalm 119:105 tells us that God's Word is "a lamp to our feet and a light to our path." What do lamps and lights do (think Maglight)? They illumine the way for us when we are not sure what is ahead. They show us the way. Lights keep us from stepping into holes. They help us avoid dangerous things that may be coming towards us. This is why the Psalmist tells us that the Word of God is a lamp and light for our lives. There may someday be a decision that faces you. Should you make decision "A" or "B"? Which is the best? Is there another direction you should take? The teaching and inspiration of the Word of God will guide you every time in making the right and best decision. The Word of God guides us.

In light of each of the above, we can see why we are encouraged to make the Word of God part of our daily lives. It is powerful. It is essential. It is filling. It is life changing. It is indispensable when it comes to growing as a Christian.

A final point about the Word of God in the life of an elder: it is absolutely impossible for a leader to authentically grow in his relationship to Jesus unless he is meeting the Lord in the Word on a regular basis. John Ortberg in his book, *The Life You've Always Wanted*, makes this statement: "I have never known someone leading a spiritually transformed life who had not been deeply saturated in Scripture."[6] Work hard to discipline yourself as a leader in the body of Christ to honor God's Word by building it into your life.

Prayer in the Life of an Elder

Every effective elder recognizes that prayer is a vital and irreplaceable practice when it comes to living his life of faith and executing his duties as a leader in the church. One of the most important things an elder can do is to pray. Conscientious elders are men who go before the Lord each day and intercede for their churches, families, and other important concerns. Elders and prayer should be inseparable.

Jesus Models the Importance of Prayer – The example of Jesus in prayer is a powerful lesson to every elder. Repeatedly, Jesus took a *blowtorch* and cut holes in His schedule to meet His heavenly Father in a time of prayer. The Gospels contain many illustrations of this priority in Jesus' busy schedule.

One of the most important things an elder can do is to pray.

Mark 1:35 states, "In the early morning, while it was still dark, Jesus got up, left the house, and went away to a secluded place, and was praying there." (Also see Matt 14:23; Mark 6:46; Luke 6:12).

It is an interesting question: If Jesus were fully God, why would He have to pray? First, the New Testament teaches us that Jesus, being fully God as well as fully man, definitely submitted Himself to the Father. Prayer was part of that submission. Jesus needed the deep connection of being with His heavenly Father while he was here on earth. He had given up the precious Presence of being with God at His throne. He needed time to reconnect and experience the Father's Presence as He willingly submitted Himself to the Father's authority and eternal plan. He needed to empower Himself for His ministry. A secondary application involves Jesus' being an example to us in the area of prayer. The focus of Jesus' life and ministry was to fulfill the plan that God had set before Him. The fact that Jesus did many things that we can imitate and follow is a plus to us, carrying many positive teaching points. The twelve saw Jesus practicing the discipline of prayer. It surely impacted them. One time they even asked Jesus to teach them how to pray (Luke 11:1). Jesus believed deeply in prayer and often practiced prayer Himself. As his followers, can we do any less?

Note — the following chapter (Chapter 3) deals with Elders and Prayer. More information is shared in that chapter on the topic of prayer.

Practical Concerns When Practicing Daily Devotion

When practicing our daily devotional time, there are several suggestions which might prove helpful in getting started and maintaining momentum.

Reading and meditating on Scripture and having a quality time of prayer are two disciplines which are intertwined. Daily, the elder, growing in his spiritual journey, takes time to fill his spirit with the Word as God speaks to him. He then turns to prayer and speaks to God. The two could be viewed as companion disciplines.

There are a couple of tried and true practical points of application that could be mentioned concerning the devotional time. When we are attempting to build these two disciplines into our lives and routines, remember these suggestions:

• *Choose a Definite, Daily Time* – For everything that is important in my life and schedule, I normally make an appointment for that occurrence. I schedule my classes at the university, dates with my wife, meetings I am to attend, and other important events. I schedule specific time for them because they are important to my life and work. So, in the same vein, I would suggest that we *schedule an appointment* with the Lord for our time together, just as we would with an important business associate or family member. It can be early in the morning, late at night, or during an open slot in the day. (I had a member of my congregation tell me that after a sermon including this point, instead of spending his entire lunch hour in the cafeteria, he began spending a half hour each day eating lunch and then going to his car in the parking lot with his Bible to meet with the Lord for the other half hour.) What time of the day would be best for you? Many leaders like the early-in-the-morning hours to meet with the Lord. Some elders tell me that mornings are not good, but the evening hours work better. Understanding that we will normally be more consistent and effective in having our devotional time when we have a specific time identified helps us with these disciplines.

Many like early morning hours to meet with the Lord; for others the evening hours work better.

• *Choose a Definite Place* – Sometimes the place we choose to meet with the Lord can be very helpful in having a successful time of devotion. This location should be one of quiet and with as few distractions as possible. It should be a private place that enables us to concentrate and focus on our purpose of meeting with Jesus there. One brother shared with me that the very best time for him was early in the morning, before his three young children were up. In his home, there were not a lot of places that afforded the quiet and focus he wanted. He began getting up early, making a pot of coffee and going to his basement which was not finished. There he had a small folding table, a light above and a comfortable chair which his wife did not need upstairs. He told me of the many times of beneficial worship and fellowship he had with the Lord there in that place in his basement which had become his personal sanctuary. Another brother told me of his plight with his four young children who were up at the crack of dawn. Arising before them was pretty hard to do. With the understanding and support of his wife, this elder found a city park on the way to his work which was fairly uninhabited at 7:00 a.m. He would park in the far corner of the park's parking lot and meet with the Lord there. He kept his Bible and prayer list in his glove box. He found that meeting with the Lord there in the park each work day provided him just the place he needed for quiet and focus.

• *Choose a (Flexible) Plan That Works for You* – When you come to meet with the Lord, it is a good idea to have a plan. (Sometimes one must scrap the plan and follow where the Lord is leading that day.) Here is a suggested approach that works well.

✝ *Begin with a brief prayer of "connection."* Clear your mind and focus on your coming time with the Lord. Ask the Lord to bless your time in the Word that day.

✝ *Your time with the Word.* There are many Bible reading plans available from your minister or local Bible bookstore. For years however, I have done the following: I have chosen a specific book of the Bible (Proverbs, Luke, Acts, Ephesians, etc.). I have read one chapter each day systemically through the entire book. After reading the chapter, I simply ask the question, "Lord, what do you want me to know, understand, and do as a result of the contents of this chapter? What message, teaching, or word do you have for me today?" When I have finished a specific book, I move on to another and continue. (There are times when I have uninterrupted time [e.g., long plane ride] that will allow me to read Romans or a Gospel or the Psalms all the way through at one sitting. It is powerful to read a book's message at one sitting.) There are many approaches to a systematic internalizing of the Word of God. The important thing is that the Word is finding its way into an elder's mind and heart on a daily basis.

† *A time of prayer.* Meet the Lord in prayer. Why not use the Lord's Prayer as a guideline and pray the elements of that prayer, expanding on them as you will. This can also be a time of intercession for others. What is on your heart that day? Bathe your family, your church, and work in prayer. Share needs and points of concern with the Lord. Use a prayer list as needed. Learn to listen when you are praying. Make your prayers a time when you connect with the Lord in a meaningful way.

Be careful not to allow yourself to drift into a rut when it comes to your devotional experience. Doing the same thing the same way day after day will lead to dullness and a lack of dynamism. Remember that God is a God of creativity and variety. Keep your devotional experiences fresh and impactful.

Day after day, the same thing in the same way, leads to dullness and a lack of dynamism.

Fellowship in the Life of an Elder

It goes without saying that fellowship (*koinonia*) is absolutely essential for spiritual development. It is not just a good idea but actually God's plan. If you read Scripture, you find that from the Trinity in the Garden of Eden in Genesis to the final pages of Revelation, our Father indicates to us that He desires fellowship with us and wants us to seriously connect with each other. God's plan for every elder is not *independence* but *interdependence*. He has fashioned the body of Christ in such a way that we are to become interdependent with each other.

The fellowship described in Scripture points us to the fact that we are to share our lives together in meaningful ways. Going way beyond the social level of conversation in the hallway before morning service begins, we are to share our lives together in deep and meaningful ways. Joe Ellis tells us, "Pour grains of sand into a bowl and they touch one another, yet remain apart. This is a description of human community. Pour drops of water into a bowl and they flow together, each partaking of the characteristics of every other drop until they are one. This is koinonia."[7]

An elder cannot make it alone when it comes to the spiritual life.

Elders and other church leaders need the strength and support provided by strong relationship bonds in the body of Christ. In relationships where trust, friendship, love, affection, accountability, and personal commitment grow, authentic spiritual development can flourish. An elder concerned with his spiritual development knows that he cannot make it alone when it comes to the spiritual life. The old adage is still true—there are no Lone Rangers in the kingdom of God. Elders need to proactively seek out and build relationships with other believers. Our relationships need to be cultivated and deepened as time passes.

There are several places that elders can discover and cultivate good relationships. The elder team itself can be a good place to cultivate these types of friendships. Members of the staff can also offer strong relationship ties. A quality Adult Bible Fellowship or Sunday School class can also provide solid opportunities to build friendships. A small group, either with spouses in a mixed small Bible study group or a same sex (all men) breakfast group can provide a time and a place to allow elders to connect with others at a deeper level.

Drawing strength, direction, help, and inspiration from others in the body of Christ is one of the main aspects to elders growing in their spiritual journeys. It is a must for every leader.

Fasting in the Life of an Elder

Fasting is a powerful discipline when it comes to leading as an elder. Fasting seems to call God's special attention to the fasting focus while also impacting the one participating in the fast. When it comes to growing closer to Christ and moving forward in our spiritual journey, fasting can and does play an important role in taking us deeper. The purpose of our fasting is all about God. He is the focus of our fasts. We fast to draw closer to Him and to connect with Him at a deeper level. We fast to express our heartfelt level of concern about the focus of our fasting issue.

The purpose of our fasting is all about God.

A working definition of fasting can be expressed in the following statement: "Fasting is the cessation from food, drink with caloric value, from people or activities for a specific period of time for the purpose of dedicating oneself to

God and His purposes." The concept of fasting in antiquity usually involved food or drink. Scripture also indicates that effective forms of fasting include fasting from people (the discipline of solitude) and, for married couples, fasting from marital relations for a time (1 Cor 7:1-7).

In Scripture, we find three types of fasts. Type number one is called the *normal fast*. The normal fast is the cessation from food and drink with caloric value, but not water (see Luke 4:1-2). Jesus practiced this form of fasting when he went into the wilderness and experienced the temptations. Type number two is called the *partial fast*. The partial fast involves withholding certain foods or types of foods for a time (see Dan 10:3). Daniel and his companions gave up certain foods for a period of time. Type number three is called the *absolute fast*. In the absolute fast, all food and liquid, including water is withheld for a period of time. This was the type of fast Paul chose when he was in Damascus waiting for the Lord's visitation from Ananias in Acts 9:8-9. (Also see Esth 4:16.)

When weighty decisions needed attention, leaders fasted.

In Scripture, fasting was employed by the early leaders of the church. When weighty decisions needed attention, when people were installed as formal leaders (Acts 14:23), and when people were sent out on missionary journeys (Acts 13:2-3), leaders fasted. Elders today should also practice this discipline at important junctures in their personal lives and in the life of the church.

Fasting is a powerful practice when it comes to growing in faith and obedience. Fasting takes us out of our normal routine and calls us to focus. Fasting should grow to be part of the life and discipline of every elder. It is a very strengthening and beneficial piece of our spiritual formation.

The spiritual disciplines discussed in this chapter are just a few that can be sought and practiced. Important additional ones should also be pursued as the journey continues for each of us. There are excellent works done on the disciplines.[8]

Reflection Question: What Spiritual disciplines do you regularly practice? Several were mentioned here. How well do you practice them? Are there other means by which you try to advance your spiritual life?

How about as an eldership? Do you practice any spiritual disciplines corporately?

Conclusion

God calls every elder in leadership in every church to move to a continuing place of depth, love, wisdom, and understanding. As an elder, I want you to be there. No more surface living. No more leading in the flesh. Heeding the call and pursuing God with all your heart is what our Father is asking you to do. Calvin Miller writes,

> It is a beautiful pursuit! How immediate it is! Spirituality is not some distant thing for which we have to struggle all our lives. It's quite the opposite, actually. It presumes that deeper living is possible because God is near. Not only is He near, He longs to empower us in a deeper way and lure us ever deeper into the splendor of our affair with Him.[9]

That is my prayer for everyone who reads this volume. I want you to continue growing to become a white-hot, God-besotted believer and servant who experiences a growing, healthy life each day in Christ. This will make you an effective leader in the church and eventually take you to heaven to celebrate at the throne of our heavenly Father.

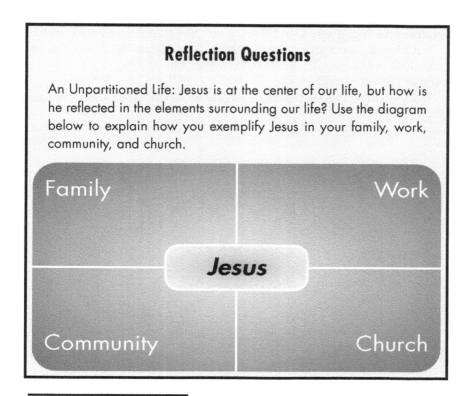

Reflection Questions

An Unpartitioned Life: Jesus is at the center of our life, but how is he reflected in the elements surrounding our life? Use the diagram below to explain how you exemplify Jesus in your family, work, community, and church.

Family

Work

Jesus

Community

Church

Chapter Two References

[1] John Henry Newman, *Apologia pro Vita Sua* (New York: D. Appleton, 1865) 57.

[2] Henry Blackaby, *Spiritual Leadership* (Nashville: Broadman and Holman, 2001) 100.

[3] Jean Fleming, *Between Walden and the Whirlwind* (Colorado Springs: NavPress, 1985) 23.

[4] Calvin Miller, *The Table of Inwardness* (Downers Grove, IL: InterVarsity, 1984) 20.

[5] Dallas Willard, *The Spirit of the Disciplines* (San Francisco: Harper and Row, 1988) 26.

[6] John Ortberg, *The Life You've Always Wanted* (Grand Rapids: Zondervan, 1997) 177.

[7] Joe Ellis, *The Church on Purpose* (Cincinnati: Standard, 1982) 66.

[8] Five of the most beneficial works on the spiritual disciplines are as follows: Richard Foster, *Celebration of Discipline* (San Francisco: Harper and Row, 1978); Dallas Willard, *The Spirit of the Disciplines* (San Francisco:

Harper and Row, 1988); Don Whitney, *Spiritual Disciplines for the Christian Life* (Colorado Springs: NavPress, 1991); Calvin Miller, *The Table of Inwardness* (Downers Grove, IL: InterVarsity, 1984); John Ortberg, *The Life You've Always Wanted* (Grand Rapids: Zondervan, 1997).

[9]Calvin Miller, *Into the Depths of God* (Bloomington, MN: Bethany House, 2000) 18.

The Elder and Prayer

David Roadcup

In the writing of a work on elders and their leadership of the church, no topic is more important or relevant than the topic of prayer. Prayer should form the heart of every elder's ministry to Christ. This chapter will be divided into two major segments: the elder and his personal prayer life and the elders and prayer in the church.

Richard Foster in his classic work on the Spiritual Disciplines writes, "Prayer catapults us onto the frontier of the spiritual life. Of all the Spiritual Disciplines prayer is the most central because it ushers us into perpetual communion with the Father. Meditation introduces us into the inner life, fasting is an accompanying means, study transforms our minds, but it is the Discipline of prayer that brings us into the deepest and highest work of the human spirit. Real prayer is life creating and life changing."[1] In an overview of all the spiritual disciplines, prayer is one of the most key and most relevant. It is by prayer that elders lead well. It is through prayer that elders connect with our Father on behalf of the church and the waiting world. Prayer is a cornerstone in the life and work of an elder. An elder must be

Prayer must characterize an elder's work and leadership. immersed in prayer in his inner man. He must also understand the critical importance of the foundation that prayer provides in the life, health, and ministry of the church.

The Elder's Personal Prayer Life

The effective elder knows that the heart of his ministry to Christ is his prayer life. Prayer must characterize an elder's work and leadership. He needs to recognize that his work and fruitfulness as a leader comes from his close relationship to Christ, nourished by effective prayer. Almost everyone knows what prayer is, but let us focus the definition for the sake of clarity.

Definitions of Prayer

In Christian literature, there are many excellent definitions of prayer which shed light on what prayer is and does. Dick Eastman states that prayer is, "Divine communication with our Heavenly Father."[2] The key word in Eastman's definition is "communication." When we pray, we are simply opening up a channel of sharing and exchange of relationship between the Lord and our hearts. St. Augustine claimed that "True whole prayer is nothing but love."[3] As we grow in our love for Jesus, we desire to be with Him and enjoy His Presence. Richard Foster admonishes us, "My first counsel is simply a reminder that prayer is nothing more than an ongoing and growing love relationship with God the Father, Son and Holy Spirit."[4] Charles Spurgeon defined prayer as "the slender nerve that moves the muscles of omnipotence."[5] God does respond to our prayers. When we pray, we touch the heart of God, and angels are dispatched to help us as the Holy Spirit continues his ministry in our lives. Martin Luther was right when he claimed, "The ancients ably defined prayer as *Ascensus mentis ad Deum, A climbing up of the heart unto God.*"[6] Authentic prayer is that which comes from one's heart to God. John Henry Newman wrote that "prayer is to the spiritual life what the beating of the pulse and the drawing of the breath are to the life of the body."[7]

Effective elders are people striving to understand prayer and its role in the Christian leader's spiritual journey. These people embrace prayer. They struggle with effective prayer in their daily lives. They experience the rough places and difficulties of building the kind of prayer life they truly want as spiritual leaders. We are all on this prayer journey together. We need to know that victory in prayer is within our grasp. We can learn the prayer discipline and grow dramatically in how to pray continuously and effectively. Emilie Griffin in her volume on prayer entitled, *Clinging,* says, "Contemplative, free, abandoned, authentic prayer is possible for every Christian, whatever his or her state in life; even in the most secular, crowded, busy, high-pressured lives, the peacefulness of prayer is a real possibility."[8]

Success in prayer is within the grasp of Christian leaders. We can grow in our prayer discipline. As hard as it may seem at times, we can move forward in this work of the heart. As leaders in the spiritual realm, having been exposed to the Word and knowing the will of God, we know we are to be fervent in prayer, and it is our heart to want to be there.

Reflection Question: Based on your experience and study of Scripture, what is our understanding of prayer? What is it? How

---

does it work? What should we expect? What does this say about your understanding of or relationship to God?

The Elder's Struggle in Prayer

I visit and work in numerous churches every year. I interact with a lot of people who are serving as elders in their congregations. I find that most elders are very sincere people who love their churches and want to serve with the highest level of excellence possible. These servants volunteer their time, efforts, and energy to provide congregational leadership characterized by commitment, wisdom, and understanding. They are genuinely good people. They believe in prayer and its power. They know they are called to pray. They also experience the same struggle most believers have when it comes to cultivating a fruitful prayer life. They experience starts and stops. They find great periods of effectiveness when prayer is regular and powerful. They also experience prayerless periods of dryness. An interesting point about success in prayer is this: in over forty-two years of ministry, I have never met one Christian who was completely satisfied with his or her prayer life! This is partly due to the fact that prayer is hard work. It involves time, focus, and concentration. Prayer calls us from our frenetic pace of activity to quiet and concentration. For many, this is not an easy task. It is a struggle for us all.

I have never met a Christian who was completely satisfied with his or her prayer life!

There are several barriers in attempting to build an effective prayer life. Some barriers are more formidable than others. Let's examine several.

Prayer and Spiritual Warfare – Why do we experience such a struggle when it comes to prayer? Is prayer really that hard? Why the huge roadblock when an open door for personal prayer presents itself? The beginning of the answer is simply: all prayer efforts are met with *spiritual warfare*. Satan does not want one elder praying with effectiveness. He knows that power is released when elders pray. He knows that portions of his strongholds are torn down when elders pray. He knows that people are led to faith in Christ when elders pray. He knows that ministers are empowered to preach life-changing sermons when elders pray. He knows that churches are fortified when elders pray. Satan trembles when groups of elders bow the knee together in prayer in a home, a church conference room, or a retreat center. Satan will do everything he can do to keep us from praying. So know that our struggle in offering regular and fervent prayer as leaders is definitely not due to a lack of self-control. It is spiritual warfare that is at hand. We must fight through the warfare and pray. Just pray. Either in our personal prayer closet or in our elder team, we pray. In our prayer efforts, we **Satan trembles when groups of elders bow the knee together.** richly bless our church and also do great damage to the kingdom of darkness. But the key is in just praying. Just begin. Just pray. Just start. As the Nike ad states, "Just Do It!" Jump in and begin. Emilie Griffin observes this struggle when she writes,

> There is a moment between intending to pray and actually praying that is as dark and silent as any moment in our lives. It is the split second between thinking about prayer and really praying. For some of us, the split second may last for decades. It seems, then, that the greatest obstacle to prayer is the simple matter of beginning, the simple exertion of the will, the starting, the acting, the doing.[9]

Richard Foster makes the critical point of stating,

We must never wait until we *feel* like praying before we pray for others. Prayer is like any other work; we may not feel like working, but once we have been at it for a bit, we begin to feel like working. In the same way, our prayer muscles need to be limbered up a bit and once the flood-flow of intercession begins, we will find that we feel like praying.[10]

When it comes to the struggle of an effective prayer life, do know that in your struggle, you are not alone. We can dramatically grow in this important discipline! Also know that in just taking the first step and beginning, just starting, is many times the key to a wonderful prayer experience.

Pragmatic Problems We Face in Prayer – There are a number of problems, difficulties, and hindrances we generally face in cultivating an effective prayer experience.

▶ *Managing Our Schedule* – The intensity with which many live in terms of schedule can be a formidable obstacle to overcome when it comes to prayer. In Chapter 2 of this volume we discuss the issue of priorities and the development of a serious plan to build into our lives a regular time for prayer. (See pages 43-44.)

▶ *Interruptions* – It is true that when we are praying, interruptions take place that draw us away from our concentration. Whether it is a knock on our door, a phone call or text message, or the cry of a child, interruptions occur. In one of my ministries, my office was in a very quiet wing of the building. I worked there all morning, through lunch and into the afternoon. I did not have one phone call the entire time. At three o'clock in the afternoon, I began a devotional time of Scripture and prayer. From three o'clock to four, I had *5 phone calls*. Some interruptions can be a part of spiritual warfare. Finding a place and time to minimize interruptions can help with this problem.

▶ *Mind Wandering* – When I lead seminars on the spiritual disciplines, at a certain point in the discussion concerning prayer, I ask the members of the audience to raise their hand if they have a problem with their mind wandering when they pray. Invariably, almost every person's hand goes up! Almost all Christians struggle with the problem of their minds wandering plus the disappointment/negative feelings that occur when it happens. I have come to several conclusions about our minds wandering when we pray. First, I believe that the Lord understands our struggle. He would rather have a sincere prayer from our hearts broken up occasionally by an unplanned mental-focus lapse than no prayer at all. Second, maintaining the mental/emotional/spiritual focus required by prayer demands a lot of effort. It is understandable that we might take an unplanned mental break during the prayer time. I do believe that the Lord is not nearly as concerned about our mental breaks as we are. After the break is over, why not come right back to where you left off and continue? You might want to think about verbalizing your prayers audibly. The idea of journaling or writing your prayers might also help with the mind-wandering problem.

The Lord is not nearly as concerned about our mental breaks as we are.

▶ *Guilt* – Guilt can present a serious problem in the flow of our prayer. If we feel we have unforgiven sin in our lives, the spiritual and emotional wall that guilt produces can keep us from connecting with the Lord. This sometimes occurs when we have been absent from prayer for some days. The very best solution is to go to the Lord in true confession, transparently, and pour out our confession to Him. First John 1:5-10 promises He is always willing to forgive us our sins. If several days have passed since prayer, crash through the wall in your spirit/mind, tell God you are back, and plunge in again. Do not let guilt at any level keep you from your connection with the Father. If your guilt is coming from unconfessed, repeated, intentional sin, why not seek out a confidant and ask for help and encouragement? Accountability will help you grow through the sin area and find a breakthrough.

▶ *Repetition* – Jesus warned that repetition is not what God wants when it comes to prayer. In Matthew 6:7, Jesus says, "And when you are praying, do not use meaningless repetition as the Gentiles do, for they suppose that they will be heard for their many words. So do not be like them." Repetition does not get it when attempting to connect with the Lord. He wants a sincere, transparent, heartfelt conversation that is meaningful in continuing to build our relationship.

▶ *Emotional Hesitancy* – Emotional hesitancy is having the opportunity with no distractions to pray and just not feeling like you want to spend the time in prayer. Possibly watching TV or doing the lawn seem more appealing to you at the moment. You haven't prayed that day, but you just don't feel like praying. If we are honest, we are willing to admit that this scenario has happened to most of us. When it happens, the very best thing to do is go to the Lord and admit that you don't feel like having prayer at that time. Don't be hesitant to do this. The Lord already knows you are feeling the way you are. The very best thing to do is to pray and say, "Lord, I really don't feel like praying now. Give me the desire *to want to want* to pray." Ask the Lord to warm you up spiritually. Listening to good praise

> **"Lord, I really don't feel like praying now. Give me the desire *to want to want to pray.*"**

music can also warm your heart and move you emotionally to seek the Lord in prayer.

Reflection Question: What is your prayer struggle? Which one of these, or another detractor, causes your prayer life to struggle? Explain why it is such a struggle.
What about as an eldership? Corporately, what are our struggles?

A Plan for Daily Prayer

Daily prayer can be done in several ways. We can effectively use a model to fashion our prayer times. We have all heard of the **ACTS** approach: **A** for **adoration and praise, C** for the **confession of our sins, T** for expressing **thanksgiving and gratitude,** and **S** for supplication, the sharing of our requests before the Lord.

We might also want to consider using the elements of the Lord's prayer in our devotions. "C.S. Lewis wrote of a practice (he thought it was his own device entirely) that he called festooning. Festooning, Lewis explained, was taking a familiar prayer, such as the Lord's prayer, and elaborating it, adding one's own intentions on at various points in the prayer until this elaboration became a ritual unto itself."[11] The Lord's Prayer (or Model Prayer) is found in two places in the Gospels. Matthew 6 and Luke 11 both record the prayer. The elements Jesus gave us to remember in prayer deal with the **things of God** first and **then the things of man.**

The Things of God
1. *Our Father in heaven, hallowed be your name* – We address our heavenly Father and begin with worship and praise.
2. *Your kingdom come* – we pray for the work of the Kingdom through the church and her influence.
3. *Your will be done, on earth as it is in heaven* – We pray for

the Lord's will to be done at all times and in every way. This can involve our church, state, nation, and our personal lives as well.

The Things of Man

1. *Give us this day our daily bread* – asking God to meet our needs and the needs of others. This part of the prayer can deal with areas of supplication.
2. *Forgive us of our sins (debts) as we forgive those who have sinned against us* – we confess our sins and genuinely ask for forgiveness. We also realize that it is the Lord's will to forgive others as we have been forgiven.
3. *Lead us not into temptation but deliver us from evil (the evil one)* – we pray for the spiritual protection for our lives and the lives of our families. We also pray protection for our church and her ministry.

Bill Hybels also offers a good approach in his helpful book on prayer. He breaks his requests down into four groups.

> I break my prayer requests down into categories: ministry, people, family and personal. Under *ministry*, I pray for the church staff, the construction programs, the public services and all the sub ministries of our church. I pray that through our ministry God will draw people to himself by confronting them with the living Christ and rescuing them from emptiness, alienation and hell. Under *people*, I pray for Christian brothers in leadership positions, the elders, the board, the sick. I pray for the unsaved people in my circle of friends, that God will draw them to himself. Under *family*, I pray for my marriage and my children. I ask God to make me a godly husband. I ask him for help with decisions about finances, education, vacation time. Under *personal*, I pray about my character. I say, 'God, I want to be more righteous. Whatever you have to bring into my life to chip away at my character, bring it on. I want to be conformed to the image of Christ.[12]

As prayer becomes a regular part of your day, be sure to look into the practices of praying Scripture, listening prayer, and the importance of silence. These are all important ways of drawing closer to the Lord and deepening your prayer experience.

Using Prayer Lists – A prayer list is an effective way to retain events, people, and other important things which might escape your memory if left unwritten. Writing down requests from friends or members of the church who have requested your prayer will help you to retain them and remind you while you are in prayer. A student of mine asked me to pray for her mother who was having surgery the next week. I had the best of intentions to pray for her mother but honestly forgot to write her mother's name on my list. A week later, the student came to me to report to me the good news of her mother's successful surgery and "to thank me for my prayers for her." Needless to say, I was sorry I had neglected to remember her in prayer. A prayer list can help us keep important things and people's needs on our prayer radar.

A warning though: If your prayer list becomes extremely repetitive and you have the sense you are in a rut, lay it aside for a time and use another approach to your prayer time. The things on your list are important, however, and returning to them a few days later will keep them fresh in your prayer regimen.

> **If your prayer list becomes extremely repetitive, lay it aside for a time and use another approach.**

An Elder's Personal Prayer Team

A prominent church leader promotes the idea that leaders in the church should surround themselves with a dozen or more people who know them, their work as elders (and ministers), and their families. The elder invites these people to join him in becoming part of a Prayer Team for his ministry as elder. Prayer Team members agree to pray daily for the elder, his family, and his work in the church. In times of stress and severe pressure when leading as an elder, his prayer team's ministry is extremely helpful. Every elder in the church should have a personal Prayer Team surrounding his ministry and work.

Reflection Question: Who would you ask to be on your personal prayer team? List them! Now, engage their service, ask them to pray for you routinely, *and* determine a way to keep them all informed of your life needs.

The Elder and Prayer in the Church

Every congregation in the kingdom should have prayer as a major part of its DNA. Prayer should be at the heart of the life of the church. Prayer should be practiced regularly and woven into the fabric of the church's experience and life.

As the spiritual leaders and shepherds of the church, elders should take the lead in assuring that prayer plays a major role in the congregation's experience. The stream never rises above its headwaters. A church's elder team **Prayer should be** (along with the paid staff and others) **at the heart of the** should take the lead in modeling, **life of the church.** practicing, and organizing for prayer.

The Early Church Models Prayer

In the Book of Acts, we see a pattern in the life of the early church that tells us that prayer was a large part of their meetings, fellowship, and congregational life.

★ Acts 1:14 – The apostles and women returned to Jerusalem and "were continually devoting themselves to prayer."

★ Acts 1:24; 6:6; and 14:23 – Prayer is significant in the setting apart of leaders for the church. (1:24 refers to the choosing of a new apostle; 6:6 describes the setting aside of the first deacons; 14:23 makes reference to prayer for the appointing of elders in churches established by Paul and Barnabas).

★ Acts 2:42 – describes the four worship practices found in the life of the church with prayer being one of the practices.

★ Acts 4:31 – tells us that the leaders of the church were threatened because of their ministry, and their response was to pray and seek the Lord.

★ Acts 6:4 – records the problem at the beginning of the early church's life involving the feeding of the Grecian widows. The apostles were challenged about the issue. They responded by pointing out that their main work in the life of the church was "prayer and the ministry of the Word."

★ Other references in Acts 8:15; 10:9; 12:5; 13:3; 14:23; and 16:25 all make reference to the importance of prayer in the life of the apostles and early church

The early church was bathed in prayer.

leaders. Prayer was an integral part of the life and practice of the early church. They prayed often and for periods of time. They modeled prayer for us today. They understood the importance of prayer, and it was a powerful practice to them. The early church prayed for power and direction, they prayed when they identified leaders and placed them in their roles, they prayed when they were facing serious problems, and they prayed when they were sending out missionaries. The early church was bathed in prayer. Our churches today would be richly blessed if they did the same.

Power and Impact through Prayer

There is no doubt that regular heartfelt prayer from pure lives makes a difference when it comes to experiencing spiritual power and results in the life of a church. Dick Eastman, a prayer giant, writes, "Where there is an absence of prayer there will be an absence of power. Where there is frequency of prayer, there will be a continuing display of God's power."[13] The bottom line on our churches and families is this: when there is prayer, things happen beyond our effective strategy and careful planning. When there is a serious lack of prayer, there is usually no power or only fair results. Prayer calls upon the power of God for our ministries and service. In this day and time of serious spiritual warfare in churches, the need to access the power of God through prayer is one of the most important roles elders and church staff members can fulfill.

Resources on Prayer
- *The Praying Church* by Alvin Vander Griend (Grand Rapids: Church Development Resources, 1997)
- *And the Place Was Shaken— How to Lead a Powerful Prayer Meeting* by John Franklin (Nashville: Broadman & Holman, 2005)
- *Giving Ourselves to Prayer— An Acts 6:4 Primer for Ministers* by Dan Crawford (Prayershop Publications)
- *The Prayer Saturated Church* by Cheryl Sacks (Colorado Springs: NavPress, 2004)
- *My House Shall Be Called a House of Prayer* by John Graf (Colorado Springs: NavPress)

Suggested Ideas for Elders in Strengthening the Prayer Life of Their Church

☞ *Prayer Team* – Every church should have a Prayer Coordinator and Prayer Ministry Team. The purpose of this team is to bring prayer to the foreground in the church's life and encourage the members of the church to grow in their belief and practice of daily prayer. This team would plan ways to offer prayer times and creative approaches in which the congregation could be involved in prayer.

A minister in Colorado preached a four-week series on prayer and fasting. He was asking them to commit to praying daily for the church and her ministry life. He also issued the invitation to every member to volunteer to fast one meal a month. In that fasting time, people were asked to pray for the church, her ministry, staff, elders, marriages, young people, and missions outreach. On the last Sunday of the series, in the foyer of the church was a very large poster with three lines on each square of the calendar page. The lines were labeled "Breakfast," "Lunch," and "Dinner." The minister asked the people to choose one meal a month for which they would fast and pray while they would normally be eating that meal. The exciting outcome was that all the lines were filled in and there were actually multiple names in many of the lined slots! This meant that every day of that month, during every meal time, someone would be praying and fasting for the life and ministry of that congregation! That's power!

☞ *Elders' Meetings and Retreats* – When elders meet, one of the main priorities of the meeting should be prayer. **Elders must lead their church on their knees.** While elders oversee the big picture of the church, they must see that biblically, their main role in the church is primarily spiritual leadership and servant leadership. Elders must lead their church on their knees, looking to the Lord for their wisdom and direction. Elder prayer times should be fervent, earnest, and passionate. The elders and staff are the primary leadership team of any congregation. They should be leading the prayer charge as the congregation moves forward.

A number of years ago, I had the great privilege to serve on a board of directors for an impacting men's ministry. This ministry literally touched the lives of hundreds of thousands of men. Thousands of men came to faith in Christ through the efforts of this work. Thousands more grew in their spiritual lives in dramatic fashion. Marriages were saved, and men were called to integrity, loyalty, and personal purity. This ministry clearly came about as a movement of the Holy Spirit. One of the things we did right when we met as a board of directors was to seek the Lord and give Him all the credit for the breathtaking results. We would meet three times a year for our board meetings. We began each meeting with a time of worship when we sang to the Lord, read Scripture to each other, and had long periods of soaking and meaningful prayer together. I will always remember those times as some of my most meaningful spiritual experiences. They were powerful and life changing. God honored the fact that we were honoring Him for our results.

Not to be too hard on chairmen of elders teams, but I have been to many elders' meetings where the team leader would call the elders together and begin by saying, "Okay, we are ready to begin. Let's have a quick word of prayer and then get to business!" I always wanted to say, "Before we 'get to business,' let's do the most important business of the evening, which is seeking the Lord on behalf of our church." While business and organizational items definitely need attention, elders should act on the fact that the most important event of every meeting is prayer and seeking the Lord. This is preeminent. Everything else, while very important, is secondary. An adage, shared by someone long ago says, *"When we work, we work. When we pray, God works!"* Because of meaningful prayer in our elders' meeting, our deliberations may go much more smoothly and we may get more business done as opposed to offering up a token prayer before we begin. Make elders meetings a time of serious, drenching prayer and intercession.

Elders' retreats are also great opportunities for serious prayer and devotion. In the retreat schedule, why not plan extended times for prayer? Depending on the schedule, these meetings can offer soaking, meaningful times for prayer and Scripture sharing.

☞ *Intercession* – Intercession is the spiritual work of praying specifically for another person and their situation or need. This concept is taught clearly in both Old and New Testaments. One of the tasks that elders are given in Scripture is that of intercession. James 5:13-16 gives instruction for elders to pray for those who are sick. Elders can also pray for a myriad of other things for their congregation members (personal problems, marriages, children, spiritual direction, etc.).

Corporate prayer by the church body is not only an imperative but absolutely essential.

☞ *Worship Services* – one of the reasons that many churches seem to lack impact may be due to the extreme lack of prayer practiced by its leaders and members corporately. Corporate prayer by the church body is not only an imperative but absolutely essential. Out of all the minutes of worship in a church's worship service(s), few are dedicated to prayer. There are opening prayers, prayers for the sick, the Lord's Supper, offering, and closing prayers. This is as it should be. But the idea of prevailing, powerful prayer is not found in most churches in their worship services.

I was invited by a good congregation who is sincerely seeking the Lord's direction in the life of their church to evaluate their Sunday services. In my evaluation, I found that out of the seventy minutes of the worship service, two minutes and fifty-six seconds were spent in prayer. Without question, there are additional important elements in a morning worship service which need to be included. But if three minutes of prayer is all that is being offered up in the ongoing life of a church when it meets, we might understand why many churches today are greatly struggling with internal problems, financial struggles, or a general ineffectiveness in reaching the lost and nurturing the saved. The elders and staff of a church can discuss this in the life of their individual congregation and should consider how this can be changed.

I was recently invited to another country to lead a national men's retreat. There were 250 men in attendance. I was excited when the leader of the service introduced one of the area ministers who was going to lead us in prayer. I prepared myself for the usual two to three minute main prayer of the evening. The young minister came to the stage and asked the audience to pray with him in a time of "suggestion prayer" (the leader suggests topics, one at a time and gives the participants time to pray about each suggestion). To my surprise, in a very interesting and passionate way, the leader led this large group of men in a prayer time that lasted 25 minutes! I found it to be a very nurturing and filling time.

As elders, can we find a way to follow the church's example in Acts and begin to incorporate serious prayer into our worship services? As elders (and staff) of the church, we need to find a way to involve our people in heartfelt and passionate times of prayer when they are meeting together. We need to seek the Lord's face in a powerful way as a body. Together, just as they did in the early church, we bathe our families, church, community, and country in prayer.

☞ *Groups That Meet* – When Ministry Teams (committees), youth groups, Small Bible Study groups, sports teams, short-term mission groups, or other groups or teams meet, they should be encouraged to make prayer an important part of their gatherings.

☞ *The Setting Apart of People for Leadership* – Acts tells us that when people were set apart for leadership (apostles, deacons, missionaries) that prayer and sometimes fasting were a part of that process. Why was this so? It was because, as discussed in Book One of **The early church did not quickly lay hands on leaders, but took their time.** this series, in the church, everything comes down to leadership. As the leadership goes, so goes the church. So the early church did not lay hands on leaders quickly. They took their time to make sure those who would be in leadership were qualified and prepared for their task.

Today, when elders are installed, when Ministry Team Leaders are put into their roles, when people are ordained into the leadership ministry, the elders should call for prayer and fasting to be part of that process. If the ordination service for the person being ordained is happening on a Sunday morning, the elders, the ministry staff, the candidate, and his family could begin a fast at dinner on the Saturday evening before, fast through breakfast, have the ordination service, and then break their fast together at a luncheon after church on Sunday afternoon.

Conclusion

In light of the need of the hour, we are calling on elders to be prayer warriors and intercessors in their prayer closets. We want you, as an elder/leader to grow in the grace and discipline of prayer. Keep struggling. Keep growing. Keep moving forward. You will win in the end. We are also calling elders to lead the church to practice and love prayer as a congregation. When God places the great period at the end of time and we are moving our flock into eternity, we will understand that to have maintained a connection to Christ and to have led our congregations to prayer had an authentic purpose—that of preparing our hearts for fellowship and connection with Christ forever.

Reflection Questions

1. How would you describe your prayer life in light of this chapter?

_____

_____

2. How would you assess the prayer life of your eldership?

_____

_____

3. What intentional plans could be made for the deeper inclusion of prayer in your life? In the life of the eldership?

_____

_____

Chapter Three References

[1] Richard Foster, *Celebration of Discipline*, 30.

[2] Dick Eastman, *The Hour That Changes the World* (Nashville: Baker Book House, 1978) 11.

[3] Richard Foster, *Prayer: Finding the Heart's True Home* (New York: Harper Collins, 1992) 1.

[4] Ibid., 13.

[5] Charles H. Spurgeon, *Twelve Sermons on Prayer* (Grand Rapids: Baker Book House, 1971) 31.

[6] William Hazlitt, *The Table Talk or Familiar Discourse of Martin Luther* (London: D. Bogue, 1848) 156.

[7] John Henry Newman, *Parochial and Plain Sermons VII* (1842–1843) 209.

[8] Emilie Griffin, *Clinging: The Experience of Prayer* (San Francisco: Harper and Row, 1984) 1.

[9] Ibid., 1.

[10] Foster, *Celebration*, 39-40.

[11] Griffin, *Clinging*, 8.

[12] Bill Hybels, *Too Busy Not to Pray* (Madison, WI: InterVarsity, 1988) 58.

[13] Eastman, *Hour That Changes*, 12.

Protecting Character

Gary L. Johnson

> *Blessed are those who hunger and thirst after righteousness,*
> *for they will be filled.*
> **Jesus Christ**

Most of us do not want to admit to this, but there is no denying it. It's the stark reality that many leaders do not finish well. Throughout our society, from the White House to the State House to the house on Main Street, many leaders do not finish well. From the ranks of businessmen, athletes, politicians, educators, ministers, etc., there seems to be a never-ending list of men who do not finish well—elders included.

Numbers support this reality. When in my doctoral program, Dr. H.B. London, of Focus on the Family, shared statistics from their organization's research indicating that many ministers do not finish well. One of their studies—from the 1990s—indicated that 50% of ministers leave the ministry by the tenth anniversary of their ordination. Sadly, that number has only increased over the years. Mark Driscoll, in *Death by Ministry*, indicates that 80% of seminary and Bible college graduates leave the located ministry within their first five years of serving. Moreover, his article indicated that an estimated 1,500 pastors leave the ministry each month due to moral failure, burnout, or conflict within the church; and that 50% of ministers' marriages are likely to end in divorce.[1] Leaders do not appear to finish well.

80% of seminary and Bible college graduates leave the located ministry within the first five years.

Names—as well as numbers—support this reality. All of us can name names of nationally recognized Christian leaders who did not finish well. Regrettably, nonbelievers can name names of Christian leaders who have fallen morally. When you and I add to this list the names of men *personally* known to us—who have fallen morally—we then reach the regretful conclusion that many leaders do not finish well—elders included. Whether because of infidelity, heresy, or various sins; leaders in the church fail to protect their character.

This is not a new phenomenon. A quick scan of Scripture reveals names of God-followers who failed to finish well. Samson had a great beginning to his life, yet his life came to a tragic end. Called by God to be a leader of His people, Samson struggled repeatedly with sexual immorality and pride (see Judges 13–16). He failed to finish well. Like Samson, Saul had a promising beginning. Anointed as Israel's first king, Saul "died because he was unfaithful to the LORD; he did not keep the word of the LORD and even consulted a medium for guidance, and did not inquire of the LORD. So the LORD put him to death and turned the kingdom over to David son of Jesse" (1 Chr 10:13-14). Saul failed to finish well.

Yet, one of the most vivid examples of a life ending in failure is that of Solomon, a man of God who was blessed beyond measure. Remember, Solomon had just taken the throne of Israel when God offered to give Solomon whatever it was that he requested. God granted him his request, and that being wisdom beyond his years—and much more. With unparalleled opportunity and resources to advance the kingdom of God, Solomon blew it—royally. When reading Ecclesiastes, it is easy to detect the misery of Solomon in his later years. His life did not have to end on such a sorrowful note. Ecclesiastes 2 reveals that Solomon tried finding fulfillment in what we can call "his five w's": wine (v. 3), work (v. 4), wealth (v. 8), women (v. 8), and wisdom (v. 9). Solomon tried it all, but in the end, he reached the conclusion that one must "fear God and keep his commandments for this is the whole duty of men" (Eccl 12:13). Sadly, Solomon failed to fear God. He failed to keep His commandments. We read in 1 Kings 11 that Solomon was not fully devoted to God in his later years of life, as his many foreign wives led him spiritually astray (see vv. 1-8). As a result, "the Lord became angry with Solomon because his heart had turned away from the Lord" (v. 9). As a leader, Solomon failed to finish well.

Why is it that men in positions of spiritual leadership run the risk of not finishing well? What causes us to fail as leaders? Noted author and seminary **What causes us to fail as leaders?** professor Dr. Howard Hendricks conducted a study of 246 men who were in full-time ministry. These men each committed sexual immorality, and after interviewing them individually, Dr. Hendricks discovered four recurring observations common to each of the men: 1) they had stopped devotionally reading the Word and praying; 2) they were not involved in any accountability relationships; 3) they were spending significant amounts of time with women other than their wives; and 4) they were convinced that moral failure could never happen to them.[2]

Reflection Question: What is the threat you face to "finishing well"? What would be the most obvious possible snare in which you may become entangled? Are they part of your personal life, church context, family concerns . . . what?

Likewise, Dr. H.B. London has repeatedly indicated that ministers often fail to finish well because they feel inadequate, isolated, and insecure. Pastors responding to surveys conducted by Focus on the Family responded by saying they felt inadequately trained to meet the ever-increasing demands placed upon them in their respective ministries. Further, the ministers felt isolated in that they did not have any close friends or colleagues in whom to confide. Finally, these men felt vocationally insecure in that they could be terminated at any moment. Moreover, their feelings of insecurity included that of their finances in that they were grossly underpaid, and had few—if any—employment benefits. Though these survey findings are from the late 1990s, they remain relevant today in that men in spiritual roles of leadership—particularly those men serving as elders—feel inadequately trained for the task; isolated from authentic and deep relationships with fellow elders; and insecure in their elder roles when difficult decisions make them the target of rejection by others.

A man may have God's call on his life to serve as an elder, and he may possess significant leadership skills, but if he does not possess—and maintain—godly character, he will not be an effective elder. Having and protecting one's integrity is leading by moral authority. For example, Billy Graham has spoken into the lives of tens of millions of peo-

| Having and protecting one's integrity is leading by moral authority. | ple around the world, including those who are world leaders. He has been the esteemed counselor |

to many sitting presidents of the United States. How has this man been so influential as a spiritual leader? He has protected and maintained his integrity.

Another example is seen in the life of the late Mother Teresa of Calcutta. Though a petite woman in size, her spiritual influence was gigantic! She spoke into the lives of many people the world over, and her significant impact was due much in part to her spiritual integrity.

Wise Up!

So then, how do we protect and maintain our moral character? Can there be a strategy by which spiritual leaders can safeguard their integrity? The answer is an unequivocal—yes! It is a twofold strategy, demanding that we both go "on the defensive," as well as "on the offensive."

Strategy #1: Know Our Enemy

We must know our Enemy if we are to go on the defensive. In 1 Peter 5:8, we are told, "your enemy the devil prowls around like a roaring lion looking for someone to devour." To know our Enemy, it's important to understand that he has personhood. He's called "the devil." Do not follow the popular trends in which people—including Christians—deny the existence of the devil, calling him merely an evil force, etc. He has personhood. He's a fallen angel bent on your destruction and mine. He is not omniscient, omnipresent, or omnipotent; for only God is that—and more! Yet, the Enemy is real and he is to be reckoned with as an adversary.

Moreover, the devil is a powerful adversary. Peter described him as a **roaring lion**, which happens to be the largest in the feline species. A roaring lion is a hungry, angry animal. Have you heard the roar of a lion? It is intimidating, to say the least. Satan has power to change his appearance. The Apostle Paul wrote that Satan "masquerades as an angel of light" (2 Cor 11:14). Paul also described him as the "ruler of the kingdom of the air" (Eph 2:2). He is a ruling angel over the fallen angels, as affirmed by Jesus when He said that there is an eternal fire "prepared for the devil and his angels" (Matt 25:41). He is a powerful Enemy—one to be respected and resisted.

Peter's description also helps us to understand that our Enemy has a purposeful plan—one that is focused on our utter and complete destruction. The roaring lion is "looking for someone to devour." The devil is compared to a hungry lion on the hunt. Its prey will be devoured, not merely injured. Having been on a photographic safari in Africa, I have seen thousands upon thousands of animals feeding in the plains of east Africa, while ever being on the alert to predators. For example, gazelles often "wake up running" as lions will be on the hunt in the darkest hours of the night, just before the dawn. In similar thought and action, we must finally wake up spiritually, and resist the enemy as he wants nothing less than to destroy our lives: our marriages, our families, and our ministry of spiritual leadership.

> **Our Enemy has a purposeful plan focused on our complete destruction.**

Our Enemy has a favorite plan, or strategy, by which to bring us down—and that is *deception*. The Apostle Paul urges us to "put on the full armor of God so that you can take your stand against the devil's *schemes*" (Eph 6:11, ital-

The Enemy's principle weapon is deception. ics mine). The Greek word for schemes is *methodia*, from which we derive our English word "methods." Our Enemy has methods for destroying spiritual leaders, and a principle weapon that he uses is that of deception. In the garden, he deceived Adam and Eve by asking, "Did God *really* say, 'You must not eat from any tree in the garden?'" (Gen 3:1, italics mine). He even tried to deceive Jesus by asking Him, "*If* You are the Son of God . . ." (Matt 4:3,6, italics mine). Jesus called Satan the "father of lies," meaning that he is the very source of deception (John 8:44). Our Enemy will do all that he can to deceive us in our thinking, all in hopes that we will compromise our integrity and fail in our role as spiritual leaders.

Reflection Question: How well do you know "the enemy," or more specifically, his tactic against you? What is he using to get into our lives?

Strategy #2: Know Our Spiritual Weaknesses

If we are to go on the defensive, we must also know the area of our spiritual weaknesses. The author of Hebrews urges us to "throw off everything that hinders and *the* sin that so easily entangles" (Heb 12:1, italics mine). The writer of Hebrews deliberately inserted the word *the* in the sentence, meaning that we are to "throw off" that one particular sin that so easily entangles us—taking us down morally. Do you know your spiritual "Achilles' heel"? What is that one weak spot that consistently trips us, causing us to tumble morally? When—and where—are we most vulnerable to this particular sin? What one area of our lives do we continually neglect? God is waiting for us to admit to this one neglected sin.

Have you ever wondered why God was so angry with Moses—so angry that He was going to kill him? We read of this moment in Exodus 4:24-26. It seems that a son of Moses was not circumcised. It was the responsibility of a father to circumcise his son on the eighth day following his birth; an expectation that God established with Abraham long before Moses was born (see Gen 17:12). Moses knew better than to neglect this one area of his spiritual walk with God. Yet, his wife—Zipporah—sensed what was wrong and she took action to right the wrong. This would not have been easy for "Mrs. Moses." It was not her responsibility to circumcise her son, who would have been far older than eight days of age. Still, it appears that she saved the life of her husband, intervening in hopes that God would not bring His wrath against Moses.

Do we have an area in our lives that is largely neglected, even to the point of bringing the wrath of God upon us? Do our spouses sense this area of moral neglect, and are they ready—and eager—to intervene because of our spiritual negligence? When will we wake up, going on the defense by admitting to that one sin that can so easily entangle us?

Not only would we be benefited by a healthy marriage by having a spouse who knows our every weakness, but also by having a brother with whom to be accountable. This is yet another way we can go on the defensive in our fight against our Enemy. Jonathan and David had more than a friendship. They established a covenant between them (see 1 Sam 18:1-4). The word covenant in Hebrew means "to chain, to fetter." So, Jonathan and David "chained" themselves to one another in deep, profound brotherhood. What mattered to God, mattered to them.

God was the very center of their friendship, and their brotherhood would extend into the next generation of their respective families. It was King David who cared for Mephibosheth, the disabled son of Jonathan.

Do we have a covenant friendship with a brother in Christ? Is God at the very center of that friendship so that

Do we have a spiritual brother who will hold us accountable?

we take most seriously our mandate to serve Him faithfully—and together? Do we have a spiritual brother who will hold us accountable, one who will ask us penetrating questions in regard to our moral character? If we do not have that man of God in our lives, pray for and find such a brother in Christ. Now, not later.

Moreover, it is essential that we go on the offensive if we are to protect our character. Far too often, we give little consideration to actually fighting "the dark side." Jesus did. Think of it this way.

Soldiers jump into LZs. They train for it, and it is full of risk when they have to do it. Some LZs are hot. An LZ is a landing zone, and when it is termed "hot," it is filled with enemy fire. There are times when Marines or men of the Army Air Cavalry are called up to deploy into a hot LZ. As the helicopter is flying closer to the LZ, the soldiers' hearts pound with anxiety, sweat is beading down from the forehead, some puke—not from the rotating blades of the helicopter, but from the turning of their stomachs knowing what awaits them the moment they jump to the ground. Battle. Instant fighting.

Jesus jumped into a hot landing zone. In 1 John 3:8, we read that Jesus came to destroy the work of the devil. That means Jesus went on the offensive. He attacked His enemy's turf, time after time. The demonic didn't stand a chance when Jesus went after them. Jesus was not a pacifist. He did not walk around in a flowing white robe carrying a handful of flowers for sale. He was a fighter, a valiant warrior, who hit the ground fighting the enemy on our behalf. He had no intention of playing it safe, or of being comfortable. Whatever it took—if even His life—He was ready to fight.

As spiritual leaders in the local church, are we fighting darkness? Have we gone on the offensive and become a threat to our Enemy—or does the devil merely laugh at us? Do we stand with one foot in Christ and one foot in the world? Do we let Satan have his way with us so that darkness most certainly clouds our thinking, and incites ungodly actions? If we have the right attitude—a sense of urgency—we will be all the more likely to take deliberate action in fighting the Enemy. Become a threat—a danger—to both him and his kingdom.

Think of it this way. Jesus said to His disciples, "I'm sending you out like sheep among wolves" (Matt 10:16). That's a picture of helpless, defenseless sheep among ravenous, determined wolves. Wolves eat sheep. Before coming to The Creek, I was a preacher in a church out in the country in Illinois. It was my first pastorate. Our sons were little boys at the time, and there was a family in the church who had a sheep farm. We would take our sons out to the sheep farm to see the lambs. Now, there were not wolves in that area, but there were coyotes—and lots of them. So, the farmer had sheepdogs—fast running and loud barking— sheepdogs. They not only chased the sheep, but they chased after the coyotes, as well. The dogs barked—warning the sheep of nearby danger. They stirred the sheep, waking them from their sleep to run towards the safety of the barn. The sheepdogs were always out in the pasture with the sheep, sniffing around with their noses up in the wind, ready for a good fight with the coyotes.

Christians tend to be mild mannered, calm, sleepy "sheep"—easy targets for the wolves, who are our demonic enemies. Too many believers have little or no capacity for fighting because we've been lulled into a pacifist mentality, thinking that all manner of violence is wrong. But consider this: we need men—elders—to become like sheepdogs among the sleepy, spiritually naïve sheep. We must have an urgent attitude that danger lurks near us. We need to be like sheepdogs, ever alert to evil around us, sniffing out the Enemy. Keep in mind that "sheepdog elders" will not be popular with people. The Apostle Paul wrote, "In fact, everyone who wants to live a godly life in Christ Jesus will be persecuted" (2 Tim 3:12). When we go on the offensive against the Enemy, not only do we protect our integrity, but we raise the bar of

We must have an urgent attitude that danger lurks near us.

character within the congregation, as well. So, be a leader who is willing—and able—to fight immorality by going on the offensive.

> **Reflection Question:** *Weakness* is a relative term; but when you read the previous material, what is the "weakest link" in your spiritual walk? Where would your spiritual life run thinnest in a time of testing?

Fight Back!

Practically speaking, I can think of two essential ways to fight our Enemy.

First, be militant in prayer. Second, be filled with the Spirit. To be militant in prayer means that we are convinced in the power of prevailing prayer, and we approach prayer as a weapon to be waged against our Enemy. When we pray in the all-powerful name of Jesus Christ, there is potency in our prayers. The Enemy knows it—and he fears it. Remember, the Apostle Paul told us that our enemy is not flesh and blood (i.e., people), but we do war with the spiritual forces of evil in the heavenly realms (Eph 6:12).

What if the Church—the body of Christ—actually fought the Enemy through assault after assault in prevailing prayer? Imagine what life would be like! Addictions would be broken. Relationships would be restored. Generosity would become the order of the day. Compassion would be rich and flowing. Families and marriages would be healed. And best of all, people—and huge numbers of them—would be saved. That's if we go on the offensive against the Evil One. Just think of the collateral damage we could do to him and his kingdom if we would prevail in prayer.

Here's a practical way to be militant in prayer. Just set the alarm on your watch or cell phone to go off at a time of day for the year it is. For example, if the year is 2009, set the alarm to go off every day for the remainder of 2009 at 2:09 PM. If the year is 2010, set the alarm for 2:10 PM. This midday alarm is a constant reminder that we are at war—and soldiers must fight the enemy if they hope to win the war. So then, wherever we are in mid-afternoon, pray! Pray militant prayers against the kingdom of evil in our personal lives, as well as in the lives for whom we care.

Our military forces use laser-guided missiles that guarantee a direct hit against the enemy. A soldier

So then, wherever we are in mid-afternoon, pray!

on the ground points a laser at a building, "painting the target." He then radios a fighter jet overhead, informing the pilot that the "target is painted." The pilot then jettisons the missile, which is guided to the target by the laser—and it's a direct hit! In a similar manner, we need to target the Enemy and his demonic forces at work in the lives of individuals, our lives included. Ask God to dispatch angels of righteousness to do battle against forces of evil around us. Mighty, prevailing prayer can enable us to protect and maintain our integrity.

In addition to being militant in prayer, be filled with the Spirit. Think of it this way. Fuel is the talk of the town. The production and price of gasoline is constantly an issue for us. Prices widely fluctuate as supply and demand fluctuates. Our emotions fluctuate as we see the prices fluctuate, making the money in our wallets fluctuate—usually downward in direction. When the price jumps sky high, people allow their gas tanks to fall very low, even allowing them to become empty. This is not only true in the States, but it is reality around the world. There is a global fuel crisis.

Moreover, there is a spiritual fuel crisis. Across the country and around the world, Christians are running on empty when it comes to spiritual power—or fuel—in their lives. Far too many elders "run on empty" when they need to be filled. How can we lead people spiritually when we ourselves are not sufficiently filled with the Holy Spirit? People often keep just enough gas in the car to get them from point A to point B; they do not have enough fuel to go the distance. In much the same way, we have just enough of the Spirit to accomplish one task at a time, instead of having a sufficient filling of the Spirit to go the distance.

Christians are running on empty when it comes to spiritual power.

Paul admonished the Church in Ephesus to not get drunk on wine, which leads to debauchery. He ordered them to "be filled with the Spirit" (Eph 5:18). In other words, get a fill up! This statement of Paul's is packed with insight from the Greek language. The phrase "be filled" is . . . 1) commanded (i.e., it is an imperative), 2) continuous (i.e., present tense—the action never stops), and 3) an issue of control (i.e., passive voice means to yield).

> **Reflection Question:** What is your spiritual LZ? How well prepared are you to engage in spiritual battle?

As elders, this command is not optional. We must be filled with the Spirit. Being that our bodies are temples of the Holy Spirit (1 Cor 6:19), we must be filled with Him continuously. As well, this command that is to be continuously obeyed is all about control. Listen carefully. Being filled with the Holy Spirit is more about being under His control than anything else. A way to tell that we are under the control of the Holy Spirit is by *cooperating with* the Holy Spirit. When He convicts us of sin, we repent. When He points out temptation to us, we say no to sin.

Moreover, living a life that is yielded to the control of the Holy Spirit (i.e., God in us) is conspicuous. Paul mentioned not getting drunk on wine in Ephesians 5:18. When a person is drunk on wine, is that person's behavior conspicuous? Absolutely! Likewise, when someone is filled with (i.e., controlled by) the Holy Spirit, is such a life conspicuous? Absolutely! The conspicuous, noticeable evidence of a person being filled with the Holy Spirit is one who lives a life marked with love, joy, peace, patience, kindness, goodness, faithfulness, gentleness, and self-control (Gal 5:22-23). Jesus said, "By their fruit you will know them" (Matt 7:16).

Spiritual leadership is demanding. Maintaining and protecting our character is difficult. We need the presence and the power of the Holy Spirit to empower us to say no to temptation, and to enable us to lead with authentic moral authority. J. Oswald Sanders, in his book *Spiritual Leadership*, wrote, "The leader must be one who, while welcoming the friendship and support of all who can offer it, has sufficient resources to stand alone, even in the face of fierce opposition, in the discharge of his responsibilities. He or she must be prepared to have 'no one but God.'"[3] Don't leave home without Him! Don't run on empty! Be filled!

Reflection Question: How can one be filled with the Spirit? What actions could you take to better provide for your own spiritual nurture?

We are soldiers fighting in hot LZs. There is spiritual war raging all around us—and we are the prize. We cannot defeat our Enemy alone. Jesus gave us His Holy Spirit to fight alongside us. Jesus gave the name "Counselor" to the Holy Spirit, *Paraclete*, meaning the "One who comes alongside." Roman soldiers went into battle two-by-two. When they were attacked, they could cover each other's blind side or back. God has sent us into a hot LZ. He has not sent us alone. The Holy Spirit—the One called alongside—can and will empower us to protect and maintain our character if we are filled with Him, and not running on empty. Get over the "fuel" crisis once and for all.

The Pentagon is the world's largest office complex. Home to the leadership of our military's five branches (i.e., the Navy, Army, Marines, Air Force, and Coast Guard), there are an estimated 23,000 people working there. In the center of the complex, there is a grassy open commons area where many of the staff eat lunch or take coffee breaks. There is even a café in this open area, aptly named the "Ground Zero Café." The café is "ground zero," as the Pentagon has been nicknamed "ground zero" by those working within its walls. Our military intelligence has determined that a majority of the nuclear missiles of our nation's enemies are aimed at the Pentagon. Hence, this one spot in our country is "ground zero." Our enemies have reasoned that if they eliminate our military leaders, they have a much greater chance of conquering our nation.

In similar fashion, our Enemy has reasoned that if he takes out the leaders of the Church (i.e., the elders), he has a much greater chance of conquering congregation after congregation. In other words, as elders—we are "ground zero"! We are marked—targeted—men. So fight for your integrity.

Be on your guard; stand firm in the faith; be men of courage; be strong.

Chapter Four References

[1] http://theresurgence.com/mdblog_2006-05-24_death_by_ministry.

[2] Steve Farrar, *Finishing Strong* (Sisters, OR: Multnomah, 1995) 27-28.

[3] J. Oswald Sanders, *Spiritual Leadership* (Chicago: Moody Bible Institute, 1980).

Restoring Character

Gary L. Johnson

Let him who cannot be alone beware of community.
Let him who is not in community beware of being alone.
Dietrich Bonhoeffer

The coat of arms of Australia speaks volumes to those who see it. It pictures two animals that are indigenous to Australia: an emu and a kangaroo. The emu is a flightless bird that never walks backwards. Its large, three-toed feet prevent it from walking in reverse. Likewise, a kangaroo never walks—or hops—backwards as its heavy, large tail keeps it from doing so. Long ago, the leaders of Australia purposefully designed their coat of arms to declare visually that they—as a people—will only move forward. Similarly, the Church needs to do the same, particularly in the realm of restoring fallen believers. Yet, far too often, that is not the case—we keep moving in reverse. We fail at making progress in the practice of restoring the character of fallen Christians, especially those who have been spiritual leaders.

Just scan the pages of recent moral lapses and see if spiritual leaders were restored? Were they restored to positions of spiritual leadership? If not, why not? We may not be able to answer those questions with great accuracy as we do not have access to factual information. But, judging from media reports, the answer would be unequivocally, no. It appears that they were not restored to leadership in ministry. It may be that the restoration process was poorly established. It may be that the individual refused to cooperate with leaders attempting to restore his character. It may be that all the parties involved refused to cooperate with the Holy Spirit and His leading!

As we tackle this issue, we must first admit that there are consequences that accompany a moral fall. For example, if a medical doctor illegally provides prescription drugs to patients, the physician will suffer the consequences if caught and convicted. Perhaps, the individual will lose his medical license and never practice medicine again. He may be able to work in the medical field, but not as a physician. In a similar manner, perhaps a lawyer makes it a practice of bribing judges, and is then caught and convicted. There are consequences. He may be disbarred and never practice law again as an attorney. He may be able to work in the law enforcement field, but not as a practicing attorney. Likewise, a spiritual leader in the Church—an elder or minister—may experience a moral lapse in both judgment and behavior. If caught and convicted, there are consequences. He may never serve as an elder again or as a pastor, but it does not mean that his character cannot be restored or that he is to be banished from the body of Christ. Once restored morally, cannot the man of God serve as a "doorkeeper" in the house of God? While they cannot be restored to leadership, they can be restored to fellowship and to a place of modest, unassuming service. If we cannot find hope for forgiveness and mercy in the Church, where can we?

> **There are consequences that accompany a moral fall.**

Reflection Question: While it is indeed a balancing act that requires careful judgment, how does one balance forgiveness of sin with the appearance of approval of sinful behavior? How can we affirm a fallen leader without affirming the sin?
- How is this done by an individual leader?
- How is this done by an eldership?

Biblical Examples

In the Scriptures, we find examples of men who fell morally. These men were leaders. For example, Samson was a judge of the people, and he had a penchant for sensualism that eventually led to his demise. He had a great beginning in life (i.e., chosen by God to lead), but a sad end. When studying his life, we observe that Samson failed to live in community with other men of God. He failed to allow other men to speak into his life. He failed to be accountable to anyone, and the rest is history. Another example is that of Solomon, a man chosen and blessed by God to lead. Yet, he failed to do what he even wrote to his son in the book of Proverbs. Solomon failed to "guard [his] heart . . . the wellspring of life" (Prov 4:23). As a result, he had hundreds of wives of foreign nationality, and they influenced him to abandon God. As a result, Solomon's life ended on a sad note of spiritual failure. It would appear that he had no one in his life to hold him accountable. After all, a king does as he pleases. Yet, should not every man who follows God make himself accountable to other men of God, no matter what his position in life? You see, this is a powerful issue of restoration—the absolute need to be in authentic community.

Should not every man who follows God make himself accountable to other men of God?

One would have thought that Solomon would have learned something from his father's moral lapse. Perhaps, David did not speak of that tragic moment in his life with his son as Solomon grew into a man. A quick review of David's life reveals that there were paths leading to his fall—five that we can easily identify. *First,* David was in the wrong place at the wrong time. He should have been off to war with his men, as stated in 1 Samuel 11:1-3. If David had been on the battlefield, he would not have seen Bathsheba bathing.

Second, King David was idle, in that he was not focused on serving the Lord. The old saying "idle hands are the devil's workshop" fits this situation. David easily found himself tempted when he was not focused on serving the Lord.

Third, **David** was struggling maritally. A quick scan of 2 Samuel 3:2-5 reveals the names of six wives, and we can add Michal to that list—making seven wives. Then, just two chapters later, in 2 Samuel 5:13, we read that "David took more concubines and wives in Jerusalem." David was not satisfied with the wife of his youth. It is reasonable to think that having multiple wives would make for a complicated home life. Interpersonal relationships between wives would be more than stressful, jealousy would abound, and David would be the leader of a most-divided home. Moreover, "the king was not to have many wives" (Deut 17:17-20), and more than one wife is too many—if we are to follow the perfect model of Genesis 2.

Which leads us to David's *fourth* immoral path, he was struggling spiritually. Being a "man after God's own heart," David knew what the Lord expected of him. The king's scroll was to be read daily (Deut 17:17-20), and it called for the king not to have many wives; anything more than one wife is too many. We must remember that God did not mandate polygamy. It was man's doing. The marriage of one man and one woman was established by God in the Garden of Eden. Moreover, after the adulterous rendezvous with Bathsheba and the ensuing murder of Uriah, David doesn't appear to be guilt-stricken until after the prophet Nathan confronts him. Clearly, David was at odds with God through this season of life.

Finally, the fifth path leading to David's fall was his lack of accountability. By this time in his life, his covenant brother—Jonathan—had been killed in battle. Jonathan would have been the closest friend to David, who would have had the ability to hold David morally accountable. Yet again, David was king, and in his mind, the king could do as he pleased. There was no obvious spirit of accountability in David's life. So, David found himself on a veritable pathway leading to a moral lapse of judgment.

Further, David suffered lifelong consequences from this moral fall. Violence became a part of his family from that day on (i.e., "the sword will never depart from your house," 2 Sam 12:10). David's son, Absalom, attempted to overthrow his father's reign. In the process, Absalom had sexual encounters with his father's concubines (i.e., wives), fulfilling the prophet Nathan's statement in 2 Samuel 12:11-12. David experienced military defeats after he was defeated morally. David paid dearly for both his brief moment of sexual pleasure with Bathsheba, resulting in the death of his son, and for the murder of her husband. His leadership position as king was never restored to its previous grandeur and strength.

David was forgiven of his sin. This gives us great hope.

Yet David was restored spiritually to God. He was forgiven of his sin. This gives us great hope that the same chance for spiritual restoration is possible for us when we experience a moral lapse as leaders. Will there be consequences? Yes, and we may not find ourselves leading in the same previous manner, but we can find ourselves completely restored to God. Check out Psalm 51. David wrote this psalm following his moral fall. It reveals the heart of a broken man; particularly, the broken heart of a broken man. A key statement appears in verse 17: "The sacrifices of God are a broken spirit; a broken and contrite heart, O God, you will not despise." David was truly sorry for what he did. He was a broken, repentant, and contrite man of God.

Reflection Question: David's fall was indeed a culmination of these five factors. Can you reflect on these factors and how they may apply to your own life? Given the following five elements, rank them in order in which they appear in your own life as a leader (1 for high, 5 for low), with a sixth spot provided for other factors:

❑ Putting oneself in the wrong place/wrong time
❑ Idleness
❑ Marriage issues
❑ Struggling Spiritually
❑ Lack of Accountability
❑ Other: _____

_____

_____

Initiating Restoration

This is the very place where restoration begins. Far too often a spiritual leader will not have a broken and contrite heart. This will be evident by his attempts to defend his sinful actions, or to transfer responsibility for his immoral behavior to others. For restoration to happen, a man must be authentically broken, contrite, and repentant.

Likewise, for restoration to take place, such action must be genuinely desired by the spiritual leaders in the local church. Yet far too often church leaders would rather sweep the matter under the proverbial rug, or hope that the fallen brother would simply leave. Church leaders do not see the need for restoration as their responsibility. In other words, "It's not our problem."

Church leaders do not see the need for restoration as their responsibility.

In 1953, Sir Edmund Hillary and Tenzing Norgay became the first people to ascend the 29,035-foot peak of Mount Everest. They were not the last. In the 1990s, Nepal lifted its once tight restrictions on climbing the legendary mountain in order to boost tourist dollars. As of 2006, more than 2,700 people have reached the summit of the world's tallest mountain, many paying over $60,000 for the experience. One result of this commercial influx has been the erosion of the traditional moral code of mountaineering. In the rush to the top, amateurs who have paid a fortune for the bragging rights will do anything it takes to get to the summit, including abandoning other climbers. David Sharp became a casualty of this modern mentality in March of 2006. The 34-year-old engineer from Cleveland did manage to reach the summit on his own. However, he ran out of oxygen on the way back down—984 feet from the top. As he lay dying, 40 climbers passed him by, too eager to achieve their own goals to take a chance on using up their oxygen on someone else. As a result, David Sharp froze to death. According to Ed Viestrus, who has scaled all 14 of the world's 8,000 meter peaks, Sharp's death is not unique. "Passing people who are dying is not uncommon. Unfortunately, there are those who say: 'It's not my problem. I've spent all this money, and I'm going to the summit.'" This attitude has produced disgust in many climbers, including Sir Edmund Hillary. "On my expedition," he said, "there was no way you'd have left a man under a rock to die."[1]

When a fellow leader falls spiritually, it is our problem! For restoration to take place, not only must the fallen leader (i.e., elder, minister, etc.) be heartbroken, but the other spiritual leaders in the church must also have broken hearts for their fallen brother. Can you think of instances when this was not the case? Rather than help the morally fallen brother up, the leadership kept him down—as if placing their feet upon his neck as when ancient rulers were defeated in battle. The local church is often quick to pass judgment and slow to show mercy. Why is that?

Reflection Question: We all know fallen leaders, and perhaps have even experienced the effects of a fallen mentor. What is our reaction to encountering a fallen leader? What *should* our reaction be? What is our responsibility to a fallen leader?

The story of Job comes to mind. The man was crushed financially with the theft of his wealth. He was crushed emotionally with the catastrophic death of all his children—and possibly grandchildren as the deaths occurred at "the oldest son's house" (Job 1:13), an indication that he was old enough to be married and have children. Job was crushed physically, ailing with seeping sores from the top of his head to the bottom of his feet. Three friends met by agreement to go and sympathize with him, but it wasn't long before they began to judge Job. They quickly surmised that their friend's suffering had to be due to unrepented sin in his life, which was far from accurate. From the earliest

> **If restoration of a fallen brother is to take place, there are two essentials.**

moments in measured time, our human tendency is to be quick in passing judgment and slow in showing mercy.

So, if restoration of a fallen brother is to take place, there are two essentials: 1) a broken, contrite heart within the fallen brother, and 2) broken, contrite hearts among other brothers for mercy to be shown the one fallen.

A Biblical Mandate and Model

The Apostle Paul wrote of the need for us to pursue restoration of the spiritually fallen in his letter to the churches throughout Galatia. Paul wrote, "Brothers, if someone is caught in a sin, you who are spiritual should restore him gently. But watch yourself, or you also may be tempted. Carry each other's burdens, and in this way you will fulfill the law of Christ" (Gal 6:1-2). These words are both pointed and powerful. Simply put, they urge us to 1) help up and 2) hold up the one that has been caught by sin.

First, notice that Paul is speaking of believers. He begins—and ends—this chapter with the term "brothers" (vv. 1 and 18). So, when it comes to "helping up" the one who has fallen, the context assumes that the one who has fallen to sin is a fellow believer. The word "caught" means to be trapped and taken down, much like a trap that is used in hunting. When a fellow leader is trapped by a sin and is taken down from a right relationship with Jesus Christ, those who are spiritual should restore him—gently. The word "restore" is a medical term, meaning to put what is broken back into its original state. So, the fallen brother is to be put back into a right relationship with Jesus Christ— that would be restoration. The word "restore" is a present tense imperative, meaning that it is a command to be continually obeyed. It is not a suggestion or an option. It is nothing short of a stern command. God expects us to restore a believer that has been taken down morally. So then, determine to "help up" the fallen brother.

Second, determine to "hold up" the fallen brother. The word *carry* is also a present tense imperative, meaning that we are to continue holding up the struggling brother under a great and oppressive weight. The word "burdens" refers to a difficult, recurring sin that continues to weigh heavily in the man's life. So then, it is commanded of those who are spiritually strong to continually help the fallen brother to gain eventual victory over the sin that so easily entangles. This restoration will not happen effectively unless there is both a broken and contrite heart in the fallen brother, and in the brothers who are commanded to do the spiritual restoring.

Such restoration will not happen quickly, or easily. That is why we must depend on the Spirit of God to lead us in this endeavor. The command to restore the fallen "gently" means that those who do the restoring must do so in a spirit of meekness, depending entirely on God for the healing to happen. There is no room for a "holier-than-thou" attitude among men doing the restoring. Having a spirit of meekness is essential in restoring a fallen brother. Paul continued his pointed comments in verses 3-5: "If anyone thinks he is something when he is nothing, he deceives himself. Each one should test his own actions. Then he can take pride in himself, without comparing himself to somebody else, for each one should carry his own load."

Restoration is the goal of church discipline, both of which are missing in far too many church settings.

> There is no room for a "holier-than-thou" attitude among men doing the restoring.

Should an elder or other leader fall morally, church discipline is essential if we hope to restore the fallen, thereby maintaining purity in the body of Christ. For example, church discipline is essential when church leaders commit marital infidelity, embezzle or mismanage church assets, practice addictive behaviors (i.e., drugs, alcohol, pornography, etc.), abuse minors, etc. Unfortunately, sin is rampant in the church—and has been for centuries. The Apostle Paul chastised the church in Corinth for not disciplining a believer for committing sexual immorality (see 1 Cor 5:1-13). There was a church in Corinth, but "Corinth was in the church."

Not only do elders avoid exercising church discipline because it is too painful, but because they are not familiar with a possible process. Jesus articulated such a process in Matthew 18:15-20. A sinner is to be confronted by the offended party. Should the sinner refuse to confess and repent, additional witnesses are to confront the sinner, hoping that confession and repentance will happen. Yet, should the sinner still refuse to repent, the individual is to be brought before the church. The elders must oversee this essential process.

The process must begin with fervent prayer, seeking the wisdom and heart of God in this pressing matter. Then, thorough fact-finding must occur and allegations must be proven, for only then can the accused be confronted (1 Tim 5:19-20). If the individual is both broken and repentant, a restoration plan can be developed by the elders. The restoration plan must be specifically tailored to fit the circumstances and the individual involved. This is not a "one size fits all" situation. In the case of a minister falling morally, a suspension may be necessary. Further, the elders will have to discuss if such a suspension will be with pay

> **This is not a "one size fits all" situation.**

or not. In the same manner, should an elder fall morally, an immediate suspension may be necessary. Appropriate communication with the congregation is necessary to foster spiritual healing, but again, confidentiality is also essential.

Recommended Resources
- John White and Ken Blue, *Healing the Wounded* (Downers Grove, IL: InterVarsity. 1985)
- Daniel Wray, *Biblical Church Discipline*
- Don Baker, *Beyond Forgiveness* (Portland, OR: Multnomah, 1984)
- David Roadcup, "Church Discipline," *Essentials of Christian Practice* (Joplin, MO: College Press, 1992)

Each one of us is one step away from stupid. Think of it this way. Football fans fell in love with Michael Vick when he played during his college years and then was selected by the Atlanta Falcons in the first round of the NFL draft. Overnight, Vick became a multimillionaire, and he played stellar football for the next five years of his professional career. He was selected for the Pro Bowl three times and ended up being offered a new contract worth $130 million. But, at the end of a dismal season for the Falcons, Vick made the mistake of responding with vile "hand language" to the booing fans and shouted, "Boo this!" That stupid moment cost him thousands of dollars in NFL fines and a public apology. Yet, it was not long before Michael Vick ended up pleading guilty before a federal judge for having an illegal dog-fighting operation at his home—being found with 66 dogs on his property. He had to pay a big price for being stupid. Vick apologized "for all the things that I've done and that I've allowed to happen." He went on to say, "I've got a lot of time to think about my actions. Through this situation I have found Jesus."[2] Each of us must know the very area of our lives where we are most vulnerable to a moral lapse.

One sure way to fail in restoring a fallen brother is in thinking that oneself is morally superior. When we think that such sin will never happen to us, our own moral lapse is certain to take place. Verse 5 does not contradict verse 2. Paul used a different word for "load" than he did with the word "burden." Verse 5 is a call to be responsible in living a Christian life, faithfully fulfilling our duties as followers of Jesus Christ.

Keep in mind that confidentiality is absolutely essential in every dimension of the restoration process. Particularly, if the morally fallen individual is a staff member, there are personnel issues and employment laws that will need to be observed. Still, no matter who the fallen brother is, we must work to restore him in an environment of sincere confidentiality. Try putting yourself in this situation. Should there be a moral lapse in your life, would you want people throughout the church and community to know the "nitty-gritty" details of your moral failure? Probably not.

Because the fear of going to the dentist is so pervasive, Japanese scientists have created a special robot that enables dentists in training to learn how to be more sensitive to the pain of their patients. If the dental trainee tugs too hard on a tooth or hits a nerve, the robot actually reacts to the pain. In fact the five-foot-three robot has been programmed to say "It hurts" and to frown when it feels uncomfortable. "Because it's so real, dental trainees can see patients' feelings and will be able to develop good skills as they treat it not as an object, but as a human being," says Tatsuo

Matsuzaki, an official at robot maker Kokoro Company. "The point is that we can share people's pain without hurting people. Treatment technique is important, but it's also important to feel what it's like to be a patient."[3] We need to try to "feel the pain" of what a fellow, fallen leader is going through. When a brother falls morally, we need to try to empathize with him (i.e., his hurt on our hearts), and when we do so, we will be far more likely to treat the situation with extreme confidentiality.

My brothers, if one of you should wander from the truth
and someone should bring him back, remember this:
Whoever turns a sinner away from his error will save him from death
and cover over a multitude of sins.

James 5:19-20

Reflection Exercise

Based on this chapter, as an eldership, draw up a procedure for dealing with the restoration of a fallen leader. Such a procedure should provide step-by-step instructions regarding not only the discipline dimension of restoration, but the nurturing activities toward this individual.

Chapter Five References

[1] "The Crowd on Mount Everest," *The Week* (6-30-06) 13.

[2] Kenny Luck, *Fight* (Colorado Springs: Waterbrook Press, 2008) 47-50; CNN.com "Vick Pleads Guilty, Apologizes," 8/29/07, www.cnn.com/2007/US/law/08/27/michael.vick/index.html.

[3] David Slagle, Decatur, Georgia; source: Yahoo News Online, "Humanoid Robot Teaches Dentists to Feel People's Pain" (11-28-07).

Exemplary Character (Stewardship)

James Riley Estep, Jr.

It is the meeting every and any church leader would want to avoid. Your congregation faces a financial crisis, but more than this, the crisis was caused by the financial mismanagement of a member of the ministry staff. The meeting is inevitable. Someone has to address the congregation, explain the circumstances, and provide a plan for reclaiming the financial stability of the church. Most meetings like this are where blame is affixed, the buck is passed, defensive postures are taken, and unilateral requests are made for the congregation's unquestioned support; reflecting a character of fear, distrust, and disconnect toward those sitting before them. Rather, this meeting takes on an unexpected tone. The Chairman of the elders explains how the elders have assumed responsibility for the situation. They dealt with the personnel issue; they have *personally* committed financial support to underwrite the church's immediate needs, have *personally* secured loans to replace the congregation's missing funds, and have established a new guideline for overseeing church finances headed by the more financially astute members of the eldership.

What a difference! It is during times of crisis that one's character as a leader is more evident. Our true priorities, commitments, and values sur-face. An exemplary eldership is one that reflects the integrity of stewardship of God's Kingdom,

> **It is during times of crisis that one's true priorities, commitments, and values surface.**

wherein others see in their leaders' lives a genuine commitment to God's church.

Elders lead by example. Ideally, they are to exemplify not only a life of a mature disciple in Jesus Christ, but a life of integrity as a leader. We should be able to say with Paul, "Follow my example, as I follow the example of Christ" (1 Cor 11:1). While there is more to leadership than character, it is an essential requirement for those who assume the mantle of leadership within the church. What is often misunderstood is that this life-quality is not one claimed by the elder, but is a description of his character affirmed by others. It is not that the elder is claiming to be blameless, but that others perceive that quality in their life. The blameless character required of elders raises the essential idea of integrity, wherein thoughts, words, values, and deeds are in harmony. He is not the "double-minded" man of James 1:8, but presents a consistent Christian witness to those within the congregation and community.

The exemplary nature of an elder's character is so important, that Paul even includes measures to preserve it from unfounded allegation. Paul not only described the character of an elder in his epistle to Timothy, but in 2 Timothy 5:19 asserts that an elder's character cannot be called into question simply on the word of one individual, but only by two or more. The elder must be a man of such exemplary character that no room for rumor is given in regard to his life.

Exemplary eldership is one of integrity. It is not only having a life of integrity, but leading with it. For example, what elders ask of others, they have already personally committed themselves to do. They cannot approve others and call others to do something they are not doing or unwilling to do. If elders are to lead with an exemplified integrity, it becomes a matter of stewardship. This chapter will first address the biblical basis of stewardship as a principle of life and leadership, and then apply it to stewardship of time, abilities, and resources.

Biblical Model of Stewardship[1]

The concept of stewardship rests on the conviction that we are the owners of nothing, and God is the Creator and Owner of everything. The Psalmist declares, "The earth is the LORD's, and everything in it, the world, and all who live in it; for he founded it upon the seas and established it upon the waters" (Ps 24:1-2). God's ownership of His creation, including us, is not a benign idea. As Christian leaders, we are to exemplify God's ownership in our lives. Paul expresses this idea in Romans, writing, "If we live, we live to the Lord; and if we die, we die to the Lord. So, whether we live or die, we belong to the Lord" (Rom 14:8). We are not our own, we are His. God's ownership is the basis of our stewardship.

Because God is the owner, we are but stewards of what He has entrusted to us. Perhaps the best biblical portrait of stewardship is found in Jesus' parable of the talents (Matt 25:14-28).[2] The message is simple, but profound. The servants are *not* the owners, but are those entrusted with the owner's possessions. Just as each servant was given a different proportion of the owner's wealth, the assessment of their stewardship was based on what they had been given. All those who were faithful stewards received the same commendation from the owner, regardless of the amount with which they had been entrusted. "His master replied, 'Well done, good and faithful servant! You have been faithful with a few things; I will put you in charge of many things. Come and share your master's happiness!'" (Matt 25:21,23). The only servant to be condemned is the one who exemplified a poor relationship with the owner (Matt 25:24-25) and exercised poor stewardship with what was entrusted to him (Matt 25:26-30). As elders, you are entrusted with God's church, and He expects you to be good stewards of His people.

Oftentimes, when we hear the word *stewardship*, the first image is tithing and church donations. However, stewardship is far broader than mere financial considerations. It is an image of ministry as well. "So then, men ought to regard us as servants of Christ and as those entrusted with the secret things of God. Now it is required that those who have been given a trust must prove faithful" (1 Cor 4:1-2). In this passage, Paul describes a servant as being an entrusted one, *oikonomos*, denoting a steward or manager of a household, often a trusted slave. A steward is responsible for something not his own, belonging to another.

Stewardship is far broader than mere financial considerations.

Stewardship also requires accountability. They are like two sides of the same coin. Stewardship without accountability is hollow, and accountability without stewardship is meaningless. Paul's relationship with the elders exemplifies this sense of accountability. For example, Luke records,

Stewardship without accountability is hollow, and accountability without stewardship is meaningless.

"The next day Paul and the rest of us went to see James, and all the elders were present. Paul greeted them and reported in detail what God had done among the Gentiles through his ministry" (Acts 21:18-19). Paul was indeed accountable to the elders of the Jerusalem church for his conduct as a minister, and accordingly he gave a report, as he had in Antioch previously (Acts 14:26-27) and during the Jerusalem council of Acts 15, wherein the apostles and elders of the churches gathered to assess the legitimacy of Paul and Barnabas's gentile mission. Peter, too, echoes this sense of accountability in ministry as a "fellow elder" when he appeals to the elders to "be shepherds of God's flock" (1 Pet 5:1-2). Stewardship is not only an individual character trait, but one practiced corporately through the principle of accountability. An elder must not only be a good steward, but an eldership must hold one another accountable for their stewardship.

The biblical portrait of stewardship acknowledges God as the owner of everything, our responsibility of serving as stewards of God's possessions, and that stewardship is a dimension of ministry. In this regard, an elder is a steward of God's Church, and his character must exemplify it.

Stewardship of Time

I always enjoyed going to Disney World's "Carousel of Progress," depicting the development of modern conveniences from the turn of the 20th century through today. Each period showed the innovations of the era, from the advent of electricity to the arrival of the digital age; each one claiming to provide timesaving devices. But, what are we doing with the time we are saving? We are also surrounded by time-keeping devices. Clocks on our computers' desktops, cell phones, wrists (watches), clocks on the wall and in the car; all conveying the notion that we can keep better track of time. Nonetheless, are we making better use of our time? Are we being stewards of the time God has given us? Do we use the time we have saved and the time we have tracked to improve our service to God, or for more leisure?

> **Are we being stewards of the time God has given us?**

Once again, we may not consider time a matter of stewardship until we acknowledge that God has given life to us, and the time of our life is in His hands. Paul warned the Ephesian Christians, "Be very careful, then, how you live—not as unwise but as wise, *making the most of every opportunity, because the days are evil.* Therefore do not be foolish, but understand what the Lord's will is" (Eph 5:15-17). James likewise cautioned the Christians to recognize the limitations of time. "Now listen, you who say, 'Today or tomorrow we will go to this or that city, spend a year there, carry on business and make money.' Why, you do not even know what will happen tomorrow. What is your life? You are a mist that appears for a little while and then vanishes. Instead, you ought to say, 'If it is the Lord's will, we will live and do this or that.' As it is, you boast and brag. All such boasting is evil. Anyone, then, who knows the good he ought to do and doesn't do it, sins" (Jas 4:13-17). The time of our life is limited, and as congregational leaders, we must be good stewards of God's time-provision given to us.

Time is the one resource that is truly both limited and irreplaceable. We are all constrained by the hours of the day, days of the week, and weeks of the year. Regardless of

Time is the one resource that is truly both limited and irreplaceable. who we may be, or what social status we may have, time is ticking away. An elder whose character does not reflect the stewardship of time may appear to be lax or even lazy, one who seems to lack purpose in what he does, or even one who is unimpressed by the priorities of ministry in the church. For example, since he does not appreciate the limited nature of time, delaying action on an important ministry decision is wholly acceptable and even routine, since he believes we have more time than needed.

How can we be good stewards of our time? Stephen Covey, world renowned leadership expert, addresses this in his book *First Things First*. He speaks of leaders working in quadrants.[3] The quadrants exist on two scales, important vs. unimportant and urgent vs. not-urgent. These form four possible combinations, and hence form a quadrant of leadership. In his studies of effective leadership, Covey regards the most effective leaders live in Quadrant 2, the important but not-urgent category. When applied to an eldership, this may include activities regarding strategic planning, meeting and project preparation, building relationships, devotional practices for spiritual formation, and even reminding themselves of the congregation's mission and core values. All of these are of the highest importance, but lack the urgency of a crisis or pressing problem.

There will always be urgent/important matters, such as a congregational crisis or unanticipated events, and no one can escape the busywork of the unimportant/not-urgent, such as wading through junk mail. However, the greatest challenge of an elder's stewardship of time is the avoidance of Quadrant 3. Covey describes this quadrant as a "Phantom" of Quadrant 2.[4] Whereas in Quadrant 2 a leader is most effective and productive, Quadrant 3 will simply keep him busy, but not that effective or productive. For example, have you ever felt like you've served at the church all week, but didn't really accomplish anything? You could readily complain about the amount of work, the busyness of the week; but could not identify one actual change and outcome of all the work? If elders are to be stewards of their time, they have to commit to preserving Quadrant 2 activities while avoiding or minimizing Quadrant 3 when possible, leaving a little time for crises and junk-mail. Intentionally prioritizing Quadrant 2 items, or at least not letting them be pushed aside by urgency or routine business, is one way to promote stewardship.

Reflection Exercise

Reflect on the last 24 "waking" hours: Write the activities into the appropriate quadrant. In what quadrant did you spend most of your time? What percentage of time in Quadrant 2?

	Urgent	Not-Urgent
Important	1	2
Unimportant	3	4

Figure 6.1

Stewardship of Abilities

While the church is far more than a volunteer organization, its ministry for the most part is fulfilled by the dedication of volunteers; individual Christians who give of their own abilities aside from their careers or homes. Their character exemplifies the stewardship of abilities, a willingness to commit to something that is deemed important; so much so that they would commit to it without pay, compensation, or even direct personal benefit. Their character reflects the biblical principle of stewardship in that they recognize that their personal abilities belong to God and they are to use them in the service of His people.

Such character exemplifies their relationship with God and a commitment to excellence in all they do. For example, Paul writes, "Whatever you do, whether in word or deed, do it all in the name of the Lord Jesus, giving thanks to God the Father through him. . . . Whatever you do, work at it with all your heart, as working for the Lord, not for men." (Col 3:17,23). The character of an elder, as a leader in a congregation of volunteers, must exemplify this stewardship of abilities if he is to lead and serve others. Yes, serving as an elder *is* a form of volunteerism, but the question is "What do you bring to the eldership's table?" What abilities do we bring to the leadership team of the church, and how is that ability recognized by the congregation?

> **The character of an elder must exemplify stewardship of abilities.**

What if an elder is never seen stepping up to the plate? What if an elder is perceived as lazy, or unwilling to use his abilities for the advancement of the Kingdom? What if he displays an attitude of "Well, I hope they don't expect *me* to do that!" while openly expressing the expectation for others to do it? An elder who seems to be disengaged with the ministry of the church, not an active servant in the church, may be setting a poor example to the congregation, making it more difficult to motivate others to commit to volunteering.

Oppositely, what if an elder is seen as being overcommitted? Continuously engaged? An elder who was always there for everything in **If he overcommits himself he becomes an example of a workaholic.** the church? If he overcommits himself, serving in every capacity on every occasion, he becomes an example of a workaholic, or even worse, eventually a burnout. While this may be seen as commendable, it in fact is devastating not only to the elder, but also to those in the congregation who may be deprived of the opportunity to serve and utilize their talents.

Either of these would not reflect exemplary character. Actually, they would be poor examples, with either one potentially debilitating a congregation. If we are to be exemplary leaders, our character must reflect the *stewardship* of our abilities. In this regard, an elder must seek a balance in how he serves. Remember, it is the stewardship of *our abilities*. To defer to Dirty Harry, "A man's got to know his limitations." You are only accountable for the abilities you possess, and the appropriate use of them. You cannot do everything. Reflecting a character of stewardship means people see you developing and utilizing your abilities for Kingdom service, not assuming responsibility for solo-serving the entire Kingdom.

Stewardship of Resources

Ah, it finally comes to finances. Unashamedly, *yes*. Like previous examples of stewardship, God does expect us as leaders in His church to reflect a character of stewardship in terms of our own personal and congregational resources. I am reminded of the feeding of the 5,000 made possible by a young man who demonstrated godly stewardship of his five *small* loaves and two *small* fish (John 6:9). As in the parable of the talents, as elders we are stewards of the financial resources God has given to our homes and congregations. This is implied in the qualification for elder, "He must manage his own family well and see that his children obey him with proper respect. (If anyone does not know how to manage his own family, how can he take care of God's church?)" (1 Tim 3:4-5), which not only refers to his family relations, but also the financial affairs of his home.

Scripture expects a Christian, and in particular the leadership of the church, to put money in its proper perspective. Paul compares the godly leaders of the congregation as those being "not a lover of money" (1 Tim 3:3d) while the false teachers in Ephesus are described as "lovers of money" (2 Tim 3:2; cf. Heb 13:5). Similarly, Peter cautions elders to be "not greedy for money" (1 Pet 5:2) as they discharge their ministry within the congregation. All of this echoes the teaching of Jesus himself who observed, "No one can serve two masters. Either he will hate the one and love the other, or he will be devoted to the one and despise the other. You cannot serve both God and Money" (Matt 6:24).

An elder's material commitment to the congregation must go beyond just giving a meditation for the offering. He must set the example for being a significant giver, with tithing as only a starting point. An elder cannot just announce the needs of a capital campaign or benevolent request, but the eldership must be among the first to step to the plate to provide for it. In fact, it has been a personal experience of my own, as well as similar instances shared with me, when an elder was virtually demanding that the congregation contribute more to the church general fund, while the elder making the request was in fact not giving to the congregation at all! This is hardly exemplary character, and in fact surfaces a deep character flaw. As stewards of our God-given resources, we must make every effort to set the example for all those around us.

This does not mean we need to adopt the practice of the Pharisees of announcing every gift with fanfare. We can be the widow with her two coins (Luke 21:1-4). Individuals simply need to see their leaders financially committing themselves to the congregation. They perhaps need to be reminded that the elders act as legal trustees of the church.[5] Perhaps an occasional mention from the pulpit or a routine financial announcement could simply note that the elders consider the financial needs of the church and step up to the plate in response to it.

This is literally an occasion where an elder must put his money where his mouth is. An elder cannot be faithful to God's instruction on tithes and offerings nor can he uphold this expectation to the congregation if in fact he himself is not practicing it. An elder must exhibit an exemplary character in terms of his financial support for the church. This is not a minor matter, but a major concern for an elder as a congregational leader. How can he set the example of financial stewardship and commitment to the congregation if he is perceived as being stingy or holding out on God? Ten percent, in the United States, is the *minimum* tip for a waiter or waitress! In all candor, a 10% tip is considered insulting, and usually denotes dissatisfaction on the part of the patron.

An elder must exhibit an exemplary character in his financial support for the church.

Has God disappointed us? Is this it? Surely God deserves better than a tip!

I remember having a conversation with a new Christian. We had been discussing the responsibilities of a new Christian to the congregation (and vice versa), one of which was financial support, specifically tithing. After class he came up to me, wanting to ask a question in confidence. He said, "I'm new to this whole Christian thing. Never had gone to church, neither did my family. What is *tithing*?" I was a bit sheepish. Money discussions are always difficult for me. But, I simply said, "In the Bible, the principle of tithing means we give one-tenth of our income back to God." I awaited his response with some trepidation, but was more than relieved when he said, "Oh, that's all?" "Well, . . . yes." "Ok, sounds good," and he walked away. He had not been programmed to be negative, respond with disgust, or become offended. He was a new Christian and this was just one more part of his life he would have to surrender to Christ.

An elder must be a tither, and then some. It is not simply a matter of church finance, but a matter of exemplary character on the part of the elder as a leader. If an eldership fails to uphold God's standard of tithing so as to avoid the issue, they are unfaithful to Him; if they fail to practice tithing while upholding it, they are unfaithful to the congregation and hypocritical. The practice of tithing causes us to practice greater stewardship of our money: since we are preserving 10% for God, we become much more conscious of where the remaining 90% is spent, rather than being frivolous.

In addition, resources does not just mean give-more-money. How do you use your home? Is it treated like a personal residence, or understood as something God has blessed you with and can be used for ministry, such as a small group Bible study? The character of an elder who demonstrates stewardship of resources simply means he acknowledges that what he has belongs to the Lord, and that he is tending to it, not using it frivolously or haphazardly. He is recognized for having the character of giving and using his blessings as a blessing for others.

Conclusion

Stewardship has a spiritual dimension to it. I could go through life thinking wholly on a horizontal level. My time, my abilities, my resources, viewing everything from a terrestrial, earthbound view; the here-and-now. However, stewardship reminds me of the vertical dimension: putting God's perspective into my perspective. What does He want me to do with my time, abilities, and resources? That distinction is reflected in our character as leaders in God's kingdom.

Stewardship involves putting God's perspective into my perspective.

The character of an elder should reflect the spiritual quality of stewardship. Those in the congregation and community should see standing before them men who reflect a commitment to the congregation, demonstrated through the quality of their use of time and abilities, as well as the commitment of their personal resources to the ministry of the congregation. Stewardship recognizes the need to strike a balance in life, to be a good caretaker with all that God has blessed His people.

Reflecting the character of stewardship in your life is the difference you alone can choose. The English alphabet has twenty-six letters, but with it you can choose to write a Shakespearian play or spray graffiti on an overpass. A piano has eighty-eight keys, but with those keys you can learn to play a piece from Mozart or continue pounding out chopsticks. God gave all of us 24 hours in a day and 7 days in a week, we can use them for His eternal purposes, or waste them on something temporal and self-serving. All of this is a matter of stewardship. It is not wishing for more, it is using what you have for the glory of God and the advancement of His Kingdom.

Remember, no one is perfect, including elders. Stewardship not only applies to the four areas previously mentioned, but is also required in the balancing of those areas in our lives. A good caretaker knows what is needed for the appropriate set of circumstance. We must be good stewards even of our stewardship.

Reflection Questions

1. Think of someone you regard as an exemplary leader, one whom you may one day aspire to be. What is it about that person that makes him a leader? More precisely, what is it about that individual's character that enables him to lead? How can this be applied to your role as an elder?

2. Do a 15-minute test on time management. On a random day, simply write down what you are doing every 15 minutes. At the end of the day, reflect on the day's events. Analyze how much time was spent working, playing, watching tv, on the computer, with your family, etc. How much time was wasted?

3. In terms of stewardship of your leadership, write in order of highest to lowest, your stewardship of the following: time, abilities, and resources. Explain your rating. What would you have to do to improve the "lowest" item? How might your fellow elders work with you to become a better steward of what God has entrusted to you?

Item	Ranking	Comment
①		
②		
③		

4. Tithing Test: Pull out your checkbook for the previous month. Total up your expenditures. Now, categorize the expenses, for example, housing, food, entertainment, insurance, etc. Make sure one category is church, including tithes, offerings, gifts, anything that you gave to the church. Now that you have the month's expenses categorized, calculate the percentage of your month's expenses given to each of the categories. Answer the following questions:

➤ What percentage is the church receiving?
  >10%   10%   <10%
➤ What is the largest expense category?
➤ What percentage is entertainment?
➤ What percentage is "optional" or "miscellaneous"?
➤ What could be shaved from other categories to increase the tithing category?

Chapter Six References

[1] Cf. James Riley Estep, "A Theology of Administration," *Management*

Essentials for Christian Ministries, Michael Anthony and James Riley Estep, eds. (Nashville: Broadman and Holman, 2005) 47-48.

[2] Please note that the term talents refers to a monetary unit, not one's personal abilities and capabilities.

[3] Stephen R. Covey, *First Things First* (New York: Simon and Schuster, 1994) 36-39.

[4] Ibid, 38.

[5] I realize that some churches have adopted the practice of creating the office of trustee separate from the elders and/or deacons; however, this is unnecessary. What the law regards as trustees is adequately paralleled with the biblical concept of elder. See James Estep, "Thus Saith the Board," *The Christian Standard* (February 23, 1992) 6-8.